Praise for *Indie Book Publishing from Start to Finish*

"At last, a comprehensive guide to the nigh-incomprehensible world of publishing! This frank yet encouraging overview is so much more than a simple handbook. Rather, it is a road map of today's publishing industry writ large. Indie professional Christina Kann ventures where few editors dare to tread by exploring the various available paths to publication, from the Big Five traditional houses to online do-it-yourself platforms to the ever-evolving hybrid model. Among concise explanations of what to expect from book production, printing, marketing, and distribution, this guide examines how different types of publishers approach each phase, allowing authors to determine which path is the best fit for them. Whether you're aiming for the NYT bestseller list or just want to create a special gift for your grandkids, Kann has accomplished what few publishers are willing to try: she has explained how book publishing actually works."

—Catherine H. Simpkiss, senior editor, Brandylane Publishers

"Any writer lost in the maze between writing their manuscript and publishing their book will want Christina Kann's comprehensive publishing guide *Indie Book Publishing from Start to Finish: It's Going to Be Awesome!* to find their way out. A mix of seasoned industry insider and fun tour guide who knows the complex terrain of the publishing world like the back of her hand, Kann equips her reader with step-by-step instructions for navigating the endless decisions publishing requires. I can't think of a single question Kann doesn't answer for writers who want to share their work with the world. I will recommend this book to each of my writing students ready to take the next step."

—Valley Haggard, director of Life in 10 Minutes
and author of *The Halfway House for Writers*

"Writing, publishing, and marketing a book can be an overwhelming and confusing process, especially for a first-time author. Christina Kann has provided a helpful, detailed resource to help authors understand the steps along the way. She shares her experience with humor and fun, and you'll enjoy the practical guidance she provides on each page of her new book. Christina Kann is a champion for authors everywhere!"

—Becky Robinson, author of *Reach*, founder
and CEO of Weaving Influence, and host of
the Book Marketing Action Podcast

Christina Kann

INDIE BOOK PUBLISHING

FROM START TO FINISH:
It's Going to Be Awesome!

WILDING PRESS

ISBN: 978-1-957833-10-1
LCCN: 2023941174

Designed by Michael Hardison
Production managed by Mary-Peyton Crook
Proofread by Grace Ball

Printed in the United States of America

Published by

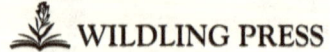 **WILDLING PRESS**

www.wildlingpress.com

This book is dedicated to Grace Ball, Michael Hardison, Mary-Peyton Crook, and Haley Simpkiss. Without y'all, book publishing probably wouldn't have stuck in my heart the way it did. I am forever grateful to you for falling in love with it alongside me.

This book is also dedicated to my dad, Steve Kann, for always making me believe that getting an English degree was like a really good idea.

CONTENTS

Dear readers,

As a child, I loved reading. My second-grade teacher would read *The Hobbit* to us at the end of every school day. The problem when I was growing up, however, was that there were very few books by people who looked like me about people who looked like me. I created the Book Bar because representation matters. When people see others like them leading and excelling in their own stories, they are invited to imagine that they are capable of the same or more. The Book Bar is a safe space, a place where marginalized voices are not the minority, where readers can see authors and characters of color on a myriad of their own adventures, telling their own stories.

And yet we live in a time when books by and for marginalized voices are being banned at an alarming rate. There are so many things going on in society that likely should be banned and are not, but we live in a world where books about human differences are somehow unacceptable. Books are a way in which to gain knowledge. They are tools that can be used to expand one's understanding and imagination. Books written in diverse voices help to provide insight into the experiences of others, and help people explore spaces and places they may not have access to. Books have the ability to save lives—whatever someone is going through, there is likely a book that can help them through that situation. There are still places within this country where people feel ostracized from their community; however, books can help bridge that gap.

When individuals in power handpick the books they want to ban according to their personal perspectives, it tells people outside of those perspectives that who they are and how they live is wrong. Books are one of the most powerful tools that exist today, and by banning them, we are disarming individuals from ever growing into healthy, empathetic, and well-rounded members of society.

The independent book industry can be a safe haven for marginalized voices. Indie stores, publishers, and authors who are not beholden to big business are able to tell, make, and sell wonderfully diverse stories. Inside indie books, every child should be able to find someone like them to aspire to, to encourage them to dream. With indie books, the narrative of the publishing industry will continue to move forward into a more inclusive future.

—Krystle Dandridge
Owner, The Book Bar

www.rvabookbar.com

Choose the Book Bar as the beneficiary
of your Bookshop purchases!

A Note from Wilding

Why did Wildling publish this book? Because we love indie publishing. When authors find the right indie publishers, that's when great, unique, important books get made and shared with the world.

But there are a lot of factors that block the road to publication for so many deserving stories. The publication process alone can be confusing and downright intimidating. Book publishing has changed so much in just the past few decades that the conversation surrounding it hasn't caught up, leaving room for predatory and monopolizing companies to control that conversation, forcing authors to decipher outdated ideas and harmful myths in their search for genuinely good advice. How is anyone supposed to make the best decision for themself and their book surrounded by all this noise?

We love indie publishing, and if you love a thing, you want to see it thrive. We want indie book publishing to prosper despite the odds against us, to move forward into sustainability despite the undercurrent of bureaucracy that pushes us back. We want to share all the information we have in an attempt to take back the conversation, to create a community of diverse, well-informed authors who can't be tricked into bad contracts or bad books—authors who can't be bullied into thinking they aren't welcome in this world. You are welcome here. Come on in.

This little book is our attempt to offer some light along the murky path. Publishing a book should be accessible to everyone who has a great story to tell, not just those with a lot of money, powerful connections, or membership in a dominant demographic. And in reality, it is! There are so many options accessible to you; you just have to know how to navigate through the fog. Maybe we can't literally hold your hand (we wish, but also, germs!), but we hope this book makes you feel less alone on the journey and more like you've got a community of independent publishers supporting you and clearing the way for you, cheering you on, pushing you and your book gently toward the joys of publication.

This guide is meant to be just that—a guide. We certainly aren't the mayors of Publishing Town. We've compiled our experience from over the years, and the experience of others in the industry, to give this general overview of what the publishing process might look like for today's indie authors. But the world of publishing is vast and complex and ever-changing, and it's simply impossible to capture what the experience is like for everyone everywhere. Use this guide in whatever way is helpful to you. And if you think we've gotten something wrong or left out something important, let us know! We are ready to update this puppy as things change or whenever we're given new information.

So, settle in and turn the pages of a book that we hope will help you publish the pages of your own.

—Mary-Peyton Crook,
Public Relations Director, Wildling Press

Introduction

So you wrote a book. Well done! That is truly the hardest part, and you've done it and now it's done. That's amazing! You might be ready to sit back and wipe your hands clean of it all, but if you want to get published, your work is nowhere near over.

From a publishing perspective, you haven't even gotten started yet. That an author has written a book is a given in the publishing world; what matters is how that book transforms in the publishing process and where it ends up once it's published. Of course, it matters that you wrote the book. But who you work with to publish your book, how they make your book better, where your book is sold, the profit you can make, and the readers who are impacted by the book also matter.

If you aren't interested in enacting someone's else's recommendations for bettering and selling your book, that's totally fine! That makes you a perfect candidate for self-publishing, and you'll still want to consider a lot of these steps along the way. On the flip side, maybe you've received an offer from a big traditional publisher. Congrats! Most of the steps of this book will take place at the publisher, and you may not get to see much of it, but this book can still serve as important context for what is happening behind the curtain. Maybe you've received a cooperative or traditional publishing offer from an indie publisher. That's awesome too! In that case, you'll definitely want to read this book carefully and take heed of the advice it has to offer.

In the end, every person who works on a book has the same goal: to share their story with others. This goal has smaller goals inside of it, like seeing a personal project to completion, earning money, making an impact on readers, and growing your platform. Keep these goals in mind during every step of your book's publication.

Also important to remember along the way is that everyone has your and your book's best interest at heart. Your publisher will only bring on your book if they believe it will thrive with them; your editor will only make recommendations to strengthen and clarify your manuscript; your designer will only design your book so it's marketable and appealing; your publicity team will only make recommendations that are likely to augment your platform. When the whole crew works together with a common goal, the end result is a beautiful, bestselling book.

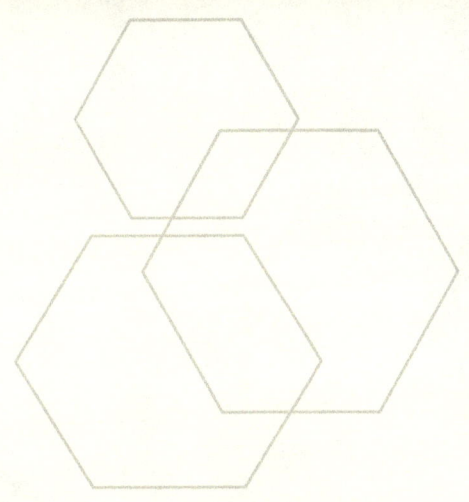

1
Before You Publish

What is a book publisher?

Don't be embarrassed! If you haven't been published, how are you supposed to know? Besides, that's why you're reading this book. Before we get into what a publisher *is*, let's cover what a publisher *isn't*.

A publisher is not a literary agent. A literary agent is someone who believes in your manuscript and its marketability, so they agree to pitch it to publishers in an attempt to sell it on your behalf. Learn more about literary agents and agencies on Page 11.

A publisher is not a printer. People ask publishers all the time if they can come in and see the books being published. Unfortunately, that's impossible, because publishers typically don't actually print the books. If you want to see a publisher at work, you'll likely be stuck watching people with glasses sending emails with stellar grammar. Learn more about printers on Pages 50, 107, and 124.

A publisher is also not an expert on law, taxes, accounting, or many of the other tangential subjects you may suddenly have reason to become interested in after signing a contract to publish your book.

FUN FACT

A publisher is also called a publishing company or sometimes a press. Additionally, there may be a single person who runs or owns the publishing company who is referred to as "the publisher," but this is not always the case.

A book publisher is a team of people who are equipped to help manuscripts grow into books. Their work is almost exclusively digital—editing Word documents, creating Adobe designs, placing book orders, running social media accounts. They work with lots of different parties—from the author to the printer to bookstores and reviewers and more—to pull the pieces of a book together and get it out on the market.

Some publishers are large monopolies like Penguin Random House, and others are quite small, like yours truly, Wildling Press. Some specialize in certain genres; some focus on specific themes; others will take on any manuscript that compels them. Some make their money through book sales, while some offer additional paid literary services to keep the lights on. Publishers can be lots of things, but more than all else, they should be your partners in publishing your book, and you should share mutual respect and enthusiasm with them.

Wrapping up your manuscript

Take a break from your manuscript

I f you finished writing your manuscript[1] yesterday, today is not the day to get published. Take a break and let it simmer before revisiting it again. Take a weekend trip. Focus on work. Read other people's books. Drink some tea. Take a walk. Do anything besides think about your book.

Why? Because writing a book is a long, hard, involved process, and odds are you've been really close to this project for a long time. You need to get some distance from it so when you do come back to it, it's with a fresh, clear, and energized mind. You still have a long way to go, and you don't want to burn out now.

Review and revise

Develop your book

When your first manuscript draft is complete, there is still more work to be done. Read through your manuscript to make sure the story makes sense. Are there any inconsistencies? Is the dialogue natural? (And are you sure? Have you read it aloud?) Does the plot make sense? Are the characters compelling (not likable; compel-

---

1 manuscript: the text of a book before it's designed into a book layout, from the moment the author starts writing it to the completion of the final proofread

ling)? Are you proud of this book? Is this a prime example of the craft of storytelling? If you answered "no" to any of these questions, keep revising until you're confident it's really strong.

Then send your manuscript to one or more trusted beta readers[2] to get their input. Your sibling who loves to read or your spouse who took creative writing in college are not ideal candidates for this process. People who are too close to you may find it difficult to convey their true opinions on what is wrong with your book, so you may not get a comprehensive review from them. You'll also want to seek out someone with more than just a passing interest in books. Find an editor, a fellow author, a passionate reader of your genre, someone from your writing class—an authority on the craft of writing and storytelling.

This is not a copy edit[3], and at this point, spelling and grammar are not a priority. A copy edit will come later, once the meat of your manuscript is more or less finalized. Be clear with your beta readers that you are not seeking a copy edit, so they should not be looking for spelling or grammar errors. When their review is complete, they should return to you a document or email listing the weak points in your book and hopefully their recommendations for improvement.

Then—and you must not skip this step—consider all of their suggestions as impartially as possible, and then enact the revisions you think are necessary. You're not required to agree with every note your beta reader provides. However, it's important to *consider*

----

2   beta reader: *a person who will read your manuscript draft and provide feedback on areas that could be strengthened*

3   copy edit: *a close edit for spelling, grammar, and mechanics*

every note your beta reader provides, and be honest with yourself. If your beta reader says your dialogue is stilted, and your immediate response is a defensive "No, it isn't!"—calm down and look at it again. Try reading it aloud. (Have I mentioned you should read your dialogue aloud?) Get a second opinion.

Work and rework those areas that need strengthening until you're really happy with your manuscript. You want to be confident that your story is as strong as you can get it without professional help. (Of course, soon you'll be seeking that professional help to take it to the next level.)

Edit your own manuscript

You simply must! For an acquisitions editor[4] at a publishing company, it's really disappointing to receive a manuscript submission that the author has clearly not even read through once themself. They'll know you skipped this step if you have glaring typos or formatting errors. They'll also know you didn't finish this step if you submit a manuscript that still has edits in Track Changes (Page 57) left unresolved. Don't make the acquisitions editor sad. You want them to be happy when they read your manuscript, because then maybe they'll publish you!

It's a good idea to review for grammar and mechanics[5]. If you're not sure what goes down in a copy edit, skip ahead to our section on copy editing (Page 63). Your publisher will provide you with an

---

4 *acquisitions editor: an editor at a publishing company who is responsible for assessing manuscript submissions and making decisions on whether and how to publish them*

5 *mechanics: punctuation, spelling, and capitalization*

editor who will make sure your manuscript gets scrubbed clean, but it makes a really excellent first impression to submit a manuscript that demonstrates your proficiency in the English language—or whatever language you're writing in.

Final review

Read it one last time

Are you getting tired of your manuscript yet? It won't help to mince words here: get used to it. Your manuscript will improve each time you review it, and you'll be reviewing it many more times with your editor. When you think your manuscript is in perfect condition, read through it one last time. We bet you'll find at least an error or two you didn't notice the first fifteen times.

Make someone else read it one last time

Honestly, you've been working really closely with this project for a long time. Have you ever stared at a word so long that it ceased to carry any meaning and became just an abstract jumble of letters? You might be missing some obvious stuff. Better even than rereading it yourself is getting someone else to read through it. You don't want to take advanced-level editing advice from your friend who teaches high school English or likes to read a lot—that's what a professional editor is for—but they might be able to catch that you misspelled "misspelled" on the first page. (It has two Ss! So hard to remember!)

Getting ready to query

Agent or publisher?

Before you go any further, decide if you are going to query[6] to get an agent to represent you, or if you're going to go straight to a publisher.

Starting with an agent

A literary agent typically works for a literary agency, and their job is to pitch an author's book to a publisher more effectively than the author could themself. Agents have connections to editors at large publishing houses, including the Big Five, as well as insight on which of them are interested in which genres and themes. They will prepare your manuscript and other materials to meet the high

---

THE BIG FIVE

Penguin Random House, Hachette Book Group,
Harper Collins, Simon & Schuster, and Macmillan
(Sometimes people include Amazon's
self-publishing arm as a sixth "big" publisher.)
The Big Five used to be the Big Six, and by the time you read this, it may
be down to the Big Four or even the Big Three. Eventually, it might be
the Big One, all under Amazon's umbrella. That's capitalism, baby!

---

6   query: the process of sending your manuscript and accompanying submission materials to one or more agents or publishers in hopes that they will offer to represent or publish it

standards of these larger publishers. They will also be your champion and advocate through the contract negotiation phase if they do ultimately score a publishing deal for you. They speak the language of the industry, and they have connections that you don't. Working with a literary agent can give the right author a huge leg up in getting their book published.

Some authors prefer not to go the agent route for a variety of reasons. Agents will take the process of submitting your manuscript to publishers out of your hands entirely. This might appeal to some authors, but other authors prefer to have more control over who they work with and on what terms. An agent will also take a percentage of your earnings from book sales as payment for their efforts.

Submitting directly to publishers

You can also submit directly to some publishing companies, especially independent publishers[7]. Publishers who accept unsolicited manuscripts[8] will usually post their submission requirements online, and an author should be able to submit via email and/or online form. An acquisitions editor at that publisher will review your materials, and if they like your submission, they will make you an offer directly.

FUN FACT

Most publishers no longer accept hard copy submissions.

7   *independent publisher: a publishing company that is not affiliated with the Big Five, Amazon, or another major corporation*

8   *unsolicited manuscript: a manuscript submission that a publisher has not explicitly requested from an author or agent*

It's then up to you to evaluate, negotiate, and ultimately accept or decline that offer.

This route doesn't appeal to some authors, as it eliminates many publishers as options. For example, an author cannot send an unsolicited manuscript directly to one of the Big Five publishing houses. The contract negotiation process can also be intimidating to some who would rather an agent handle all that for them.

Final thoughts about how to query

Both paths are valid, both have their pros and cons, and both can lead to success or failure. It's up to you to consider how you like to work and the vision you have for your book when deciding which route is the best for you.

Save your manuscript in standard manuscript format

Do your research—good job, you're already reading this book!— and then demonstrate that you've done your research. When an acquisitions editor receives a manuscript submission in standard manuscript format[9] (example on page 243), they will understand that the author is competent, committed, and conscientious.

This isn't the right time for flair; this isn't the right time to show that you're a designer in your own right. Format your manuscript using standard manuscript format with the following features:

---

9   *standard manuscript format: a generally agreed-upon set of formatting guidelines that most publishers prefer manuscripts be submitted in*

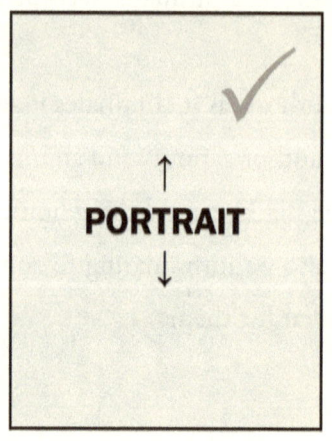
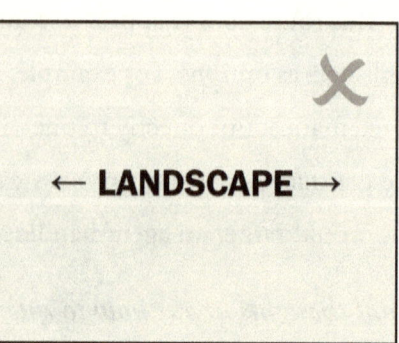

- 8.5x11" portrait page (word processors' default)
- 12-point Times New Roman or Arial font (absolutely nothing jazzy!)
- one-inch margins on all sides
- 2.0 line spacing
- paragraphs indented half an inch (using the ruler settings instead of the tab button is a huge plus!)
- left-alignment, not justified
- numbered pages (top right corner is preferred)
- scene breaks indicated by ###
- page breaks (CTRL+Enter on a PC or Command+Enter on a Mac) between chapters
- only one space between sentences

Writing and collecting your query materials

Each publisher or agent will have different submission requirements, so be sure to review those before sending anything to anyone. However, you'll definitely want to have these materials prepared before getting started:

- your manuscript, formatted in standard manuscript format
- an elevator pitch[10] of your manuscript
- a one-paragraph synopsis[11] of your manuscript
- a one-page synopsis of your manuscript
- a query letter

What's a synopsis?

A synopsis is a summary of the plot of your book. Some authors are surprised to find that one of the hardest parts of writing and publishing a book is boiling their 75k-word novel into a one-page summary. However, it's important to have a strong synopsis—and, in fact, even several different versions of your synopsis—before you start querying.

Start by writing down everything that happens in your book. This isn't a good opportunity to be jazzy and cute; your synopsis should be quick, direct, energetic, and factual. Don't sweat the small

---

10   *elevator pitch: a one-sentence summary of your book that is designed to really hook someone hearing about it for the first time in as few words as possible. If you found yourself in an elevator with a literary agent and only had thirty seconds to grab their interest, what would you say?*

11   *synopsis: summary*

stuff, and jot down enough to connect us to your main character and understand the entire plot. "Entire plot" means the full narrative arc, including the resolution. Yes, for a querying synopsis, you want to give away all the spoilers. An agent or publisher can't know if they appreciate the arc of your manuscript if they can't see the whole thing.

It's okay if you wrote down way too much on the first pass. For some people, it can be easier to write something long and then revise it down to a page. If your synopsis is longer than one page, start trimming excess description. Do we really need to spell out the whole subplot with the neighbor? Or is there other, more important information here that better describes or better sells your book? Cut, cut, cut, until you have a one-page synopsis.

It's worth noting that when an agent or publisher places a word or page limit on the synopses of their submissions, they are not making a suggestion. If they ask for a synopsis under five hundred words, and you send them a two-thousand-word synopsis, you're *only* communicating that you can't follow directions. Respect people's time and profession and submit exactly what they're asking for.

Once you're satisfied with your one-page synopsis, save it. In fact, surely you saved it before you even started drafting and have it on auto-save. Save your one-page synopsis with a very reasonable file name like Kann1pgSynopsis.docx.

Now it's time for the one-paragraph synopsis, or about a hundred words. How much can you cut from your original synopsis? What elements are the most essential to your plot, to your narrative? You want to include the title, the genre, your word count, the essential plot, and the essential theme. Some authors use comparisons like "It reads like *Iron Widow* by Xiran Jay Zhao mixed with Netflix's *Breaking Bad*," but only use this tool if you really feel it helps to accurately communicate the vibe of your book; a phrase like "The next *Hunger Games!*" isn't nearly as helpful as you'd think unless you truly managed to write a new angle on children killing each other for sport. Be as vivid and concise as you can. This is a true writing challenge, and you're up to it!

What's a query letter?

You've probably written a cover letter to accompany a resume or application for a job prospect. For many people, it's a challenge to capture the essence of why they would be a good fit for a certain position in just one page of formal, formulaic writing. A query letter is basically your manuscript's cover letter for the job of becoming a book.

A query letter (example on Page 244) should be brief, no longer than a page, and concise. Now is not the time to whip out your rambling metaphors or quippy one-liners. Imagine an agent or acquisitions editor—or, more likely, an intern—who has a pile of a hundred submissions to get through in a day. This person may at first read only the query letters from authors' submission packages to gauge their interest. Imagine you have just this one page to capture their curiosity and inspire them to read more.

A query letter should open with the manuscript title, its word count, and your elevator pitch in the first paragraph. Then your letter should go on to explain why this book is special and marketable.

The second paragraph should give a more detailed synopsis, including spoilers! This is a good opportunity to use the one-paragraph synopsis you drafted earlier.

Since you've researched the publisher or agent you're querying to thoroughly, you know exactly what they're looking for, and your book meets that need. You need to make this clear in your query letter! If you're querying to a publisher who is specifically seeking queer literature, mention that in your opening sentence. Tell them right away why they need your book—not why *you* need *them*. If they're located in your hometown, mention that. If they've published other books similar to yours, mention that. Show them you've done your homework and explain to them exactly where your book fits into their bookshelf.

> **CAREFUL**
>
> *A single queer side character does not a queer book make! If you market your book as something it's not, the acquisitions editor will figure it out eventually. If you want to be able to call your book queer, you need to commit to portraying round and varied queer characters. This applies to everything, not just queer lit! You don't get to add a single character of color and call your book diverse; you don't even get to write one character who enjoys chess and call it a chess book. Commit to your story's elements and then describe them accurately in your query.*

Wrap up your query letter with an incredibly brief summary of what you've said above, an expression of your gratitude, and an offer to send more information upon request. Most agencies will not want you to send your manuscript with the initial query, so it's a good idea to offer to send it if they're interested. Be sure to include your contact information with your signature!

Name the file something really simple and straightforward, like KannQueryLetter.docx. Don't be cute about it and risk wasting a tired editor's time.

Here's the catch: each agency or publisher will have different query requirements, so even when your template query letter is done, it's not done. You'll need to lay fresh eyes on it for every new query and adjust it to meet the publisher's requirements and brand.

Querying

Keep records

Keep track of to whom you're submitting your manuscript and when. The best way to do this is on a spreadsheet, but you could also use a Word or Google document, or even a piece of paper and a pen (not recommended).

A submissions spreadsheet record could include the following columns:

- publisher or agency
- date sent
- recipient (the name of the human person to whom you sent your query)
- method of submission (email or contact form or something else)
- notes (where you can add notes of your own—"form did not seem to confirm submission"—or notes from the company—"encouraged a follow-up after two weeks")
- follow-up date
- results

FUN FACT

Some agencies and publishers permit submission followups, and some do not. Some even tell you exactly how long you need to wait before you follow up. Be sure to do your research and follow each company's guidelines!

Keeping track of these details will help you avoid submitting to the same person or company twice. It's also a good way to keep your information in one place so whatever you need, it's there when you need it.

Simultaneous submissions

Some publishers might ask when you submit, "Is this a simultaneous submission?" They're asking if you're also submitting this manuscript to other publishers or agents at the same time you're submitting to them. Don't let this question alarm you—you absolutely *should* be sending out simultaneous submissions to many agents or publishers at the same time. If you get asked this question, answer honestly: yes, you are sending simultaneous submissions.

This is kind of like applying to college. If you apply to only one college, there's a very real chance you will not get accepted, and since you opted not to apply to other colleges, now you're just not going to college this year. You want to apply to several colleges, including some reach schools as well as some you're fairly confident you'll get into, so you have options depending on who accepts you.

Read the requirements!

We have already mentioned twice that every publishing company and literary agency will have different submission requirements, so skip this step at your own peril! Find each company's submissions page and read the requirements carefully. One may require a three-page synopsis, while another won't accept anything longer than a page. One may require all materials as separate attachments;

another may require all materials be pasted into an email's body. One may require the entire manuscript, another might require the first ten pages, while another might not open any submission that has any portion of the manuscript attached. Some might even ask for your CV or online portfolio!

Remember that you are not any kind of exception here. These agents and editors don't know you, and you don't want their first impression of you to be that you can't follow the rules or don't do the required reading. Start strong with a good impression by making sure that you have followed their unique guidelines to a T.

Craft the query

Some publishers and agents may accept queries over email, but you'll find that many have a website submission form to simplify the process for them. If you find both a submission form and an email, opt to use the submission form to make things easier for them to process. Very rarely (read: almost never) is there a submission so extraordinary that it cannot be submitted through the website form.

Carefully pull all the required materials together in your email or the website submission form. Some agencies or companies might prefer for the query letter to be in the body of the email, so there's your whole email right there. Well done! If they prefer to receive the query letter as an attachment, write a simple, one-paragraph email that includes the title of your book, an invitation to consider it, and an offer to send more information or clarify any issues, and then attach your query letter separately.

Attach whatever needs to be attached—don't skip anything! Acquisition editors and agents don't have time to hunt down your missing attachment or sift through the three separate emails you had to send because you messed up the first one. They will likely opt to skip your submission instead, possibly without informing you that it has been rejected.

When the email is ready, review it. Carefully. Maybe even review it again.

Then . . . send!

Then . . . wait.

EMAIL PRO TIPS

When crafting an important email like this, put the recipient's email address into your email form last, after you've written and reviewed the email and its attachments. This will prevent you from accidentally sending the email before it's done.

If you use Gmail, include the word "attach/attached/attaching" in the body of your email (ex. "I'm attaching my cover letter here."). Gmail will warn you if you've said you're going to attach something but are trying to send the email without an attachment!

Waiting

As Tom Petty and the Heartbreakers once said, "The waiting is the hardest part." Agents and publishing houses receive hundreds and sometimes thousands of submissions annually. Their slush piles[12] are tall. It can take months for them to get back to you—if they get back to you at all.

Some publishers and agents will state on their website, "We will only respond to submissions we're interested in." If you don't hear back, it's because they're passing on your manuscript. This is another reason why it's so crucial to send simultaneous submissions: if you only send your submission to one publisher, they may never get back to you, and you'll be left just runnin' down a dream (incidentally also a Tom Petty and the Heartbreakers song).

Some publishers and agents will include follow-up instructions on their website. Some may prohibit following up entirely, while others might invite you to follow up if you haven't heard back within a certain amount of time. Most will completely prohibit following up via the phone, so any follow-ups will likely be made via email.

This is a great time to pull out your spreadsheet again, where you've noted publishers' and agents' follow-up instructions and can log when you do so.

Rejection

You've probably heard all the stats before. Stephen King's *Carrie* was rejected by eighty publishers before it was accepted by Doubleday (now owned by Penguin Random House). C.S. Lewis was rejected eight *hundred* times before publisher John Lane accepted *Out of the Silent Planet*, Lewis's first novel.

---

12 *slush pile: the queue of submissions an agent or publisher has yet to evaluate. This term comes from the olden days, when they'd have real towers of actual paper manuscripts stacked all over their offices. Now, the slush pile refers to the digital queue of submissions.*

You are going to be rejected.

Probably a lot.

Receiving a rejection of your manuscript submission is truly part of the journey to ultimately getting it published. Agents and acquisitions editors are picky, so read each rejection as more of a "this isn't for me" than a judgment on the objective quality of your book. For every hundred agents who don't connect with your book, there is one out there who will really believe in it. It's a numbers game, so just keep going.

When (not if) you receive your first rejection, remember C.S. Lewis and his eight hundred rejections. You only have 799 to go!

Contract negotiation

Amazing! You received eight hundred rejections, and then you finally received a publishing offer or an offer of representation[13] from a literary agency. Congratulations! We know it wasn't easy, but you did it. Now, the hard work begins: contract negotiations. Legal writing is decidedly *not* the same as book writing, so buckle up.

Getting an offer from an agent

If you've been querying directly to agents, an agency may make you an offer of representation. If you like what they have to say in this offer, they will send you a contract proposal. This is not a guarantee that your book will be published; it is a guarantee that the agency will try to get your book published. You will sign a contract directly with your agent, who will in turn try to get you a publishing contract with a publisher. If they succeed, you will then have two contracts.

Remember that a contract is a draft by one party that is meant to be negotiated between both (or all) parties. Your agent will send you a contract that was written to benefit them. It will be tempting to jump right on any offer, but be sure to review the

13   *offer of representation: an offer extended by a literary agent to represent the author and the manuscript when querying the manuscript to publishers on the author's behalf*

contract carefully, ask questions, and make requests for revisions as you see fit. Don't hesitate to consult a lawyer if you'd like a professional opinion—just be sure to hire someone who has experience with literary agencies and book contracts. A divorce lawyer will likely not be familiar with the ins and outs of the publishing industry.

Your contract with your agent will likely cover what they plan to do to develop your book, what you might be expected to do to develop your book, how they will query it to publishers, and what commission they will take should your book sell (usually around 15%). It will also include the terms for getting out of the contract; although all parties hope to never have to discontinue a contract, if the necessity arises, it's important that everyone is already on the same page.

If everything goes well, this contract with a literary agency could mark the beginning of a long and lovely relationship. Take this process seriously, review the contract carefully, and only commit when you're very confident all parties will be satisfied.

Getting an offer from a publisher

If you've skipped the agent portion of our show, you may receive an offer directly from a publishing company, possibly from the same person who made the decision to publish your book. Whereas a contract with an agent will focus more on the relationship between the agency and the author, a contract with a publisher will focus much more closely on book production and royalty [14] structure[15].

If you didn't skip the agent portion of this process, your agent might be bringing you these offers from publishers. If you like one publisher's offer, they will then send you a contract proposal. Read this carefully, collaborate with your agent, ask questions, request changes, and consult a professional if you would feel more comfortable doing so. Don't be afraid, and take this seriously.

A publisher will offer you one of three types of publishing deals: traditional publishing, cooperative publishing, or self-publishing. Let's explore these options a little bit more.

Traditional publishing offer

Traditional publishing is often an author's first-impulse preference. When a publisher makes a traditional publishing offer to an author, they are offering to invest one hundred dred percent of the funds required to publish your book. They may even offer you an advance on your book's royalties or an honorarium at the signing of the contract.

The reason this path would appeal to most authors is obvious. Who wouldn't want to get their book

(NOT SO) FUN FACT

Advances and honorariums on book contracts are becoming rarer and rarer as the book industry changes in the age of technology.

---

14   royalty: *a percentage of the profit that the author will earn from each book sold*

15   royalty structure: *the threshold (in number of copies) at which you start earning a percentage of the profits from your book sales, and then the subsequent thresholds at which that percentage increases*

FUN FACT

The costs of publishing a book include but are not limited to staff, technology, and printing.

published "for free"? But, of course, it's not as simple as that, and having someone else pay your way does come with its drawbacks.

A traditional publishing contract will often come with some extreme caveats. The publisher might not let an author be involved in the editing process.

Your book might change a lot once it leaves your hands, and you've signed away your right to protest. Some traditionally published authors don't even get to see their book's cover until it's being marketed publicly.

Some authors might not mind handing over their book to professionals, being told what to do, and waiting for the royalties to start accruing. But many creatives have a hard time giving up artistic control over their projects. If you're the kind of person who wants to be involved during the publishing process, a traditional path might not be for you.

Traditional publishing was at one time pretty much the only path available to authors, so it's become revered in the industry as the ultimate goal—and sometimes as the only "correct" way to get published. However, the publishing industry is changing more rapidly than the stigmas surrounding it. Many publishers, especially independent publishers, are unable to liberally hand out traditional publishing offers in today's economy. Independent publishers often rely on other publishing options.

Cooperative publishing offer

Cooperative publishing[16] involves a financial investment from both the publisher and the author to produce the book. Authors get to be more involved in the creative process and develop their writing skills, and they ultimately earn higher royalties than they would have under a traditional arrangement to help them recoup their investment.

Some old-school opinions in the publishing industry hold that an author should not have to pay to publish their book. That is simply not true anymore—not in this economy. These kinds of ideals from publishing's days of yore can seriously limit an author's chance of getting published, and of independent publishing houses publishing excellent books outside the reach of the Big Five. Cooperative publishing contracts are how smaller publishing houses can publish more books than they would be able to if they were limited by only being able to offer traditional publishing contracts.

A cooperative publishing contract will outline the author's and publisher's respective investments and responsibilities. It will delineate the author's royalty structure, as well as identify any potential additional costs. It may also include a timeline and other production details.

When you agree to publish a book cooperatively with a publisher, you're committing to being part of a publication team. You and the publisher will work together to edit, design, print, and

16   *also called "hybrid publishing," "collaborative publishing," or "subsidy publishing"*

market your book. Often, a publisher will not approve or finalize any decision without first getting the approval of the cooperatively publishing author. The publisher will do their best to balance the author's preferences with industry standards and creative excellence to produce a marketable, professional book that the author is really excited about, having been involved in the entire process.

There are also educational publishing programs that operate under the cooperative publishing model. Some publishers offer certain kinds of cooperative contracts that leave room for the author to learn about the publishing industry and grow as a writer. This expands the author's investment so it encompasses not only the production of their manuscript into a book, but also their own professional development.

Self-publishing offer

Even if you submit your manuscript for consideration for a traditional or cooperative publishing contract, you may still receive an offer to self-publish with that company rather than publish under their imprint[17]. Alternatively, an author might know from the start that self-publishing is the right path for them and skip the querying process entirely.

Self-publishing is an extremely valid path for an author to take, so consider this option carefully if it's presented to you. Lots of authors have met success by self-publishing and self-marketing their book. It's getting easier and more acceptable every day for self-pub-

---

17   imprint: *the brand name under which books are published (may be the publishing company's name, like Penguin Random House, or may be one of the publishing company's smaller imprints, like PRH's Bantam Books)*

lishing authors to create lovely books that meet or even exceed industry standards and distribute those books globally.

"Self-publishing" at one time meant an author editing their own manuscript. Self-publishing used to mean covers produced sloppily from stock imagery or depicting a friend's colored-pencil artwork. Self-publishing used to result in odd books that just didn't look "right" or "professional." Again, publishing is changing quickly in the digital age, and these prejudices could not be less true in the twenty-first century!

When an author works with a publishing company to self-publish their book, they get to tap into all the expertise and resources of that publishing house while maintaining their creative control. The publisher will serve as the "packager"[18] of the self-published book and work closely with the author to make their vision come to life. The publisher will make recommendations based on their expertise, but every decision lies with the author (outside of technical aspects of publication, which are not typically up for negotiation).

As a self-publishing author, you can print your book using the same printer the publisher uses to print books published under their imprint. IngramSpark is a wonderful self-publishing printer and distributor that allows an author to manage and monitor their sales reports and book information from the comfort of their couch at home. Through this company, your book will be available through print on demand (Page 128) all over the world.

Once the book is produced, the author will get to decide when

18   *packager: a publishing company or another service that facilitates the author self-publishing their own book. Some are full service, while others (like Amazon) are more click-it-and-get-it-done, you're-on-your-own.*

and how it's released, and where it goes from there. Finally, and most appealingly to many self-publishing authors, the author gets to keep one hundred percent of the profits made from sales of the book (in what we'd call a 100% royalty structure).

During the contract negotiation phase for a self-publishing arrangement, be sure to speak up for exactly what you want. You have the opportunity to pick and choose where you'd like publication support from the publisher versus what you might be able to do yourself. For example, if your sibling is a skilled graphic designer, maybe they can design your cover. But be realistic with yourself about what your book needs and how you envision it. If you're already investing money in your book's production, you don't want to cut corners and risk lowering the quality of your book.

Any self-publishing contract should state that all book rights remain with the author. At the end of a self-publishing process, the publisher will hold zero ownership over your book. They should earn zero money from copies sold. In theory, you should be able to take the completed book (along with its digital files) and walk away from the publisher entirely at the end of publication.

A self-publishing author can even create an LLC for their books. If you publish under an LLC that you created for the purpose of publishing books—BOOM! You're now an author who was published by a publisher. You can even help other people self-publish their books using your LLC if you want to. Creating an LLC can also be a helpful distinction when it comes to taxes and bookkeeping.

Don't be afraid to self-publish. It doesn't carry the stigma it

Traditional Publishing, Cooperative Publishing, and Self-Publishing

	Pros	**Cons**
Traditional publishing	• The author does not have to invest any money. • Larger traditional publishing houses tend to have more resources for book production and promotion. • There is a certain prestige that comes with getting published traditionally and through a well-known publishing house. • The author may receive an advance or honorarium upon signing.	• The author will likely not get much say in their book's production or promotion. • This is the most challenging type of publishing contract to obtain • If the book doesn't perform well in its first couple months, the publisher will likely stop investing in it.
Cooperative publishing	• The author gets to work cooperatively with the publisher to create a book in their vision that meets industry standards. • The author may learn something along the way.	• The author will invest funds. • Publishers who offer cooperative are often smaller and may have fewer resources to work with. • There is a stigma against authors paying a publisher to publish their book.
Self-publishing	• The author gets to keep full creative control over their book's production. • The author gets to keep all of the book's net profits.	• The author is required to navigate the entire publishing process on their own or hire someone to help them do so. • The author is responsible for troubleshooting any issues or hiring a professional to do so. • There is still a stigma against self-publishing.

once did, and thousands of wonderful books are self-published annually. For the most part, readers can no longer tell the difference between a traditionally published book and a self-published book. In fact, you have likely read a self-published book without even realizing it.

What's a royalty structure?

A royalty structure is a set of thresholds written into an author's contract that outlines exactly when they will start earning a percentage of the profits from their book sales and when that percentage will increase.

Royalty structures differ greatly across the different kinds of publishing. For example, a self-published author should receive 100% of their book's profits in a 100% royalty structure from the very beginning. A self-publishing contract would not feature tiers or thresholds; instead, the author would receive 100% of the profits from every single book sold from its inception.

On the flip side, an author who is traditionally publishing their book will see a share of their book's profits going to the publisher, who has invested a lot of time and money in this book and wishes to recoup some of that through book sales. A traditional author, for example, may not start earning royalties until a couple hundred copies have sold—especially if the author was granted an advance on those royalties, in which case they'd likely start earning royalties after their publisher has recouped that advance. Then, their royalty percentage may increase once a thousand copies have been sold. Perhaps by the time ten thousand copies have sold, the author will max out their royalties and earn 60% royalty on every book sold moving forward. Some traditional publishers won't make an author hit any threshold to start earning royalties; some publishers have different thresholds. When you see a royalty structure on your contract proposal, however, the odds are good that the publisher has sent you their standard royalty structure, or the one they send to all their traditional authors.

In between is cooperative publishing. Cooperatively publishing authors have typically invested money alongside the publisher, so it's more important that those authors are able to recoup some of their investment as well. Cooperative contract proposals may offer more in the way of royalties to their authors to help offset that financial investment.

Often, an author's royalty percentage is calculated based on the net profit made from selling a copy of the book, not the entire cost of the book. If a book is sold for twenty dollars, the gross profit is twenty dollars. But subtract the wholesale discount (around 50% of the cover price) and the cost to print (around 25% of the cover price) and you're left with about 25% of the cover price as net profit—and the author and publisher will split that net profit based on the royalty threshold laid out in the author's contract.

Sketchy offers

It's true that not all publishing companies are built the same. Some may appear sketchy, and yes, some are outright scams. It can be hard to know what you're getting into before you've gotten into it, so let's figure out how to evaluate any publishing offer to be sure that it's golden.

Vanity presses

While not all vanity presses are scams, some go about getting their business in unethical ways by misrepresenting what they do. A vanity press will publish any book if the author is willing to pay for it, regardless of its content. Some vanity presses will happily publish books that feature sexist, racist, homophobic, prejudiced, or otherwise harmful content for the right price. Less dramatically, some vanity presses will happily publish bad books, ones that simply are not good and do not merit publishing, and they typically don't invest the time it would take to improve those books to meet the industry standard.

A vanity press can look a lot like an independent press offering a cooperative publishing contract. So what's the difference between cooperative publishing and vanity publishing? A vanity publisher, as we mentioned, will publish any book for any author for the right price. A hybrid, independent publisher vets their submissions and only makes offers on those projects they enjoy and believe to be marketable. A vanity press makes their money from book production fees; a hybrid publisher uses the author's investment to produce that author's book, and then makes their money from book sales and sometimes other services, like self-publishing or editing.

How can you tell if a publisher is truly evaluating their submissions or not? There are a couple of ways you could approach this. First, take a careful look at their website. See if they talk about their manuscript evaluation process anywhere. You can also take a look at other books they've published to see if there appears to be any rhyme or reason to their choices, or if it seems they will publish anything.

You can also do some internet research to see what experiences other people have had with the same company. Look them up on Better Business Bureau. Google "[company name] scam" to see if any alarming results pop up. You can even ask in your writing groups on Facebook or your local critique group to see if anyone has experience with the company you're evaluating.

It's important to remember the biases that exist within the world of publishing during this transitional period in the industry. Lots of people still hold on to outdated ideas about publishing intended to obscure the process and gatekeep indie authors and publishers. Someone online may give a publishing company a bad online review because the company charges a fee to publish some or all of their books, when these days we know that's a perfectly legitimate way to get a good book published. (Not that this totally happened to Wildling or anything.)

It can be tough to evaluate a publishing company, but it's important. You don't want to sign a contract with a company who's already trying to take advantage of you before you even start out. Your money, your time, and your creative work are at stake here.

Self-publishing services to be wary of

Not all self-publishing support is created equal. There is an overwhelming variety in what an author can get in terms of self-publishing assistance. Some programs let you do it yourself for free through the computer; others cost thousands of dollars and guide you through every step of the process.

Some authors find real value in the free self-publishing that can be done through Amazon. Authors are totally on their own when they take this path; they must edit, design, and otherwise prepare their books for publication, or else pay professionals to take care of each step. And, yes, it's certainly possible to make a crisp, clean, sharp, professional-looking book this way!

However, the unfortunate reality is that a lot of books published for free through Amazon are the kind that give all self-published books a bad name. Some authors skip the professional edit or design their own covers to save money, to the extreme detriment of their final product. Being a skilled writer doesn't mean an author knows everything about publishing or even about books. The reason there are professional publishers is because it's a long, hard, complicated process, and not everyone knows how to get it right. Why should an author know how to publish a book? Their specialty is writing, whereas a publisher has lots of training and experience in publishing. Many authors would benefit from hiring professionals to take care of the bulk of production and guide them through the self-publishing process.

Wildling Press and many other publishers and literary companies offer self-publishing services. This path, while certainly more expensive than Amazon's free publishing, allows the self-publishing author to receive recommendations and guidance from professional book producers who publish books for their own imprints all the time.

There are also companies in between Amazon and full-service self-publishers that will package your book for you into a final, printable product. Many of these services use the upload-your-files-and-get-a-book-in-return technique, and many don't connect authors with honest people to help guide them through the process. These companies can be a step up from Amazon publishing for an author who knows what they're doing, but you still won't get the individualized help you could through a full-service publisher.

What if you don't get the offer you want?

Yikes, this is the worst. You've gone to all this effort, and you've gotten an offer that's not quite what you were hoping for. Maybe you were hoping for a traditional contract and they've offered you collaborative; maybe you were hoping to get published under an imprint but have only gotten self-publishing offers; maybe you queried your manuscript to a ton of agents but haven't heard back from anyone. What now?

First, have a conversation with yourself or someone you trust, and be real. What is most important to you? Publishing a book, or doing it a certain way? Do you have flexible funds?

Is your book's timeline important? Are you doing something wrong? Did you try an artsy query letter and now wish you'd been more professional? Is your story marketable? Are people looking for a story just like yours?

These are hard questions, and you'll want to really think about the answers to them to help you figure out the next step in your publishing journey. If you love your book and just want to see it published, if you've queried it for six months with no luck, if you've saved some money to help you get published—maybe consider self-publishing.

If your financial situation prevents (much or any) investment, if you're a writer from a marginalized group, if your story has been received well by beta readers, if you're certain this is what publishers are looking for right now—maybe hold out for a traditional offer like you originally wanted. You might want to review your submission materials or ask someone else in the industry to do so, and then consider if you can change anything to try a new approach in future submissions.

Be real with yourself. Are you, as an author, sending up red flags for people reading your submission? When they asked for a marketing plan, did you answer, "This is the publisher's responsibility."? When they asked for your one-page summary, did you send them seven thousand words in response? Did you comment something weird on their recent Instagram post? Is there a reason, a real reason, you're not getting the offer you seek?

We can't answer any of this for you. If you're not getting the offer you want, the next step is up to you. So take a break, think hard about your book, and be honest with yourself about how you might be able to reach your goals. Don't hesitate to reach out to a publisher or agent if you have questions about their processes.

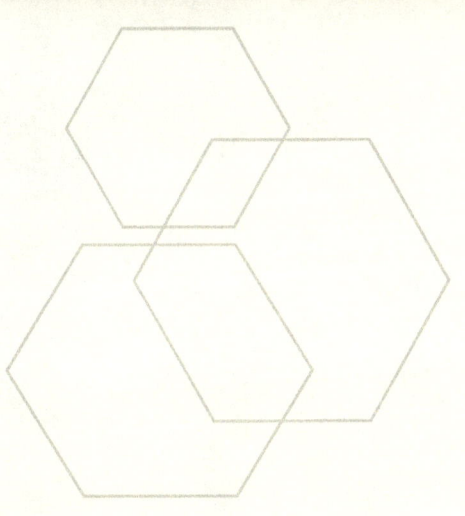

2
Producing Your Book

Getting started

Congrats! You've signed a publishing contract, and now you're ready to get started. Some things will likely have to happen before you dive into your first edit. These steps can vary greatly depending on your publisher and type of publishing contract; however, here are some things to think about as you get started.

The timeline

Typically, any book publishing agreement will have a tentative timeline laid out. A typical, 75,000-word novel may be estimated to take eighteen months or so to produce, including the six-month pre-order marketing period between when the book is completed and when it's formally launched. This timeline is one acquisition editor's attempt to predict how long each step of your book's production process will take based on past experience. Because this timeline is merely an "attempt" to "predict," it's important to keep in mind just how tentative it can be.

Your project manager and the rest of your production team will do their best to adhere to this estimated timeline. However, there are a million and one things that might slow up that process. Very, very often, the editing process takes longer than anyone expected. Sometimes, the design can take a while, especially if your book project has unique design elements like illustrations or differences from page to page.

Do you want a good book or a quick book? You hear this question all the time in the book publishing world, and the question is solid. Sometimes, authors want to skip a bunch of steps and get their book done quickly. Perhaps an author has already hired some other editor or some other cover designer. This is totally fine, and some perfectly lovely books have been produced this way. However, this author will likely be self-publishing, as publishers typically insist that books published under their imprint go through the full production process. This is how they ensure quality in each title they produce.

The bottom line is: expect your book's production to take longer than the tentative timeline laid out. It's more a rule than an exception that books take a seriously long time to make. And you've been working on this book so hard for so long—of course you want to make sure you get a good book rather than a quick book!

Getting your files together

If you've made any changes to your manuscript since submitting it or have other concerns about your file, be sure to send your publisher your cleanest, most up-to-date manuscript.

Completing intake paperwork

There can be a wide variety in the type and amount of paperwork your publisher may ask you to complete before your project gets started. You may need to complete tax or other financial paperwork to help your publisher pay you and/or get paid by you. You may need to complete some kind of questionnaire about your vision for book production and marketing so your publisher will know how to meet you where you are. You may have to provide your book's synopsis and an author bio.

Unfortunately, paperwork makes the world go round, so you're likely to see at least some at this stage. While we can't know for sure what kind of paperwork you may have to fill out before getting your book published, we can provide some advice: be honest, be concise, and turn it in on time!

Making your first payment

If you are self-publishing or collaboratively publishing your book, you'll have to pay your first production installment before you get started on anything else. Do your best to make the payment quickly and through the method your publisher has requested, and save the poor bookkeeper a headache!

Getting to know your production team

You might not get to real-life meet or even virtually meet your entire production team—or any of it, for that matter—right when your project gets started. After all, they all have other projects they're working on at the same time! Some of those may be projects they're trying to wrap up before they move on to yours. But it's still a good idea to figure out: Who works at your publisher, and what do they do?

Here's a brief overview of who might be on your production team. For more detailed information about what their roles involve, please refer to the various steps outlined in the rest of the production section.

Project manager

Your project manager will help you through the entire publishing process. They are your book production partner, and you'll work closely together to produce your book. This person will be your primary contact, and any questions or ideas you might have about your book publishing at any time should go straight to them.

Editor

Your editor will perform a copy edit on your book, and possibly a developmental edit as well. This person will be trained and experienced in using *The Chicago Manual of Style* and *Merriam-Webster's Dictionary*. They'll have experience editing in your genre. They will do everything they can to make your book sharper, clearer, and stronger. Your editor could very well be your project manager, but sometimes it might be someone else.

FUN FACT

The smaller an independent book publishing company is, the more likely each staff member is to wear more than one hat. At a larger publisher, project managers may not edit at all, but at a very small publisher, your project manager could also be your designer, your editor, the bookkeeper, or the publicist.

Proofreader

Your proofreader is another editor who will give your book one final review after its big edits. This person may be less specialized in your genre than your editor because they're pretty much exclusively reviewing for spelling, grammar, and mechanics issues. If your project manager doesn't personally edit your book, they may proofread it. The publisher may not know who your proofreader will be until the time comes, as these tasks are often distributed to whichever editor is available at the time.

Illustrator

If you're writing a kids' book, or if your book calls for illustrations for some other reason, your production team might include an illustrator. If you don't already have illustrations, your project manager will tell you when it's time to get started on those, and they'll likely be able to make some recommendations for whom you might choose. You may also work with a cover illustrator even if you're not having the interior illustrated. If you're not sure if you're going to be working with an illustrator, ask your project manager.

It's worth noting that authors working with traditional publishers on their book will likely have very little input on their illustrator and illustrations, if any. One of the benefits of working with an independent press is that authors often get to be much more involved in every step of the process, including art direction.

Designer(s)

Your designer or design team will be responsible for laying out the interior of your book as well as designing the cover. Some designers work one-on-one with authors, while others prefer to work through the project manager. After all, that's why the project manager is there! Regardless of their communication style, you can trust that your designer will make your book pretty.

And regardless of what people say, everyone judges books by their covers.

Printer

If you're publishing your book with a publisher under their imprint, you will likely not have to worry much about printing beyond placing book orders and making sure the copies you receive look correct and crisp. Your printer will likely be a company completely separate from your publisher, and they'll do the physical printing of books. You'll probably never have to interact with them, and your project manager will be able to give you instructions and answer questions about them.

If you're self-publishing, the story will be a little different. Usually, self-publishing authors get to create their own account with the printer that they'll manage entirely on their own, including uploading their own files and controlling their book's printing. This means you'll place your own book orders, make your own payments on them, report any printing errors, and perform other tasks.

Publisher

Not all publishing companies have a single person who they designate as The Publisher, but lots do. One or more of these people we've listed so far, or perhaps a separate person entirely, may be The Publisher, and they likely also own or run the company. If the publisher isn't part of your production team, you may not hear from them very often. Some publishers are like CEOs in how they run their companies, and they hire skilled staff they can trust to do the bulk of the legwork for them. Other publishers prefer to be in the trenches with their team, working on the minutiae of books for their entire career. After all, you don't get into publishing unless you love making books!

Office staff and other roles

You may also encounter your publisher's accountant or administrator when it comes to payments and book orders. You may occasionally speak to an intern or assistant when they're handling a small task on behalf of your project manager. You might receive an email forwarded from a separate e-book designer or a marketing designer. Lots of people with lots of skills work together to make a single book come to life.

Especially at a small press, one single person may certainly fill two or more of these roles. So get ready to trust your project manager to show you the way. Which leads us to our next point . . .

Let's talk more about your project manager

If you go skydiving, for your first several sessions, you have to be physically attached to a skydiving professional. Because skydiving is such a mortally risky activity, you simply are not permitted to attempt it without a professional. That person will suit you up, check and double-check your equipment, help you jump, and ensure you land safely. And, crucially, they'll make sure you stay afloat and have fun along the way.

Now, book publishing certainly isn't as high-stakes as skydiving. But that's no reason not to partner with a professional who can help you suit up, double-check your equipment, make sure you land safely, and ensure you have fun and learn something along the way. Your project manager is your skydiving pro, and you need to trust them enough to put your book in their hands.

When an author is matched with a project manager, a partnership is formed. Often, the project manager spoke up to ask for your book particularly because it interests them. Otherwise, someone else made the decision that this book would do well under this person's guidance. Usually, your project manager will have a lot of experience working on books in your genre and age group. Furthermore, they'll probably be really passionate about the genre as a reader. This means they'll have a ton of professional experience that has prepared them for this moment, when they get to take your book and make it shine.

It's crucially important that an author is able to trust their project manager to make decisions that are in their book's best interest and offer sound, professional advice. It's just as important that a project manager can trust the author to accept critique humbly, try their best to develop their craft, and trust them. Yep, the project manager has to trust that the author can trust them. And furthermore, the rest of the production team—the designers, the publisher, the accountant, everyone—has to trust that the project manager is doing their job correctly and building a lovely book.

As you can see, a lot of trust goes into the production of any book. It can be hard to put your book into someone else's hands and then listen to what they say you should do with it. Of course that's hard. You've been working on this book for so long and put so much of yourself into it, handing it off might feel wrong. But it's not. Eventually, you have to send your child to school, because you can't teach them calculus. That's not your job. You're not a mathematician (probably). Your job was to birth them or adopt them and nurture them and help them develop and get them to school age in one piece. But you have to send them to school if you want them to become an adult, if you want them to understand calculus. And you have to trust that the school system can do that. In exchange, the school trusts that you haven't raised an unteachable goblin child.

<u>Edits</u>

If your manuscript needs developmental work on character, plot, or structure, your first edit may consist primarily of general suggestions for you to consider and then enact on your manuscript wherever is needed. If extensive developmental work isn't required, your first edit will likely look very red with grammar and spelling corrections when you open the file. You might experience both general notes and a detailed redlined edit.

Don't panic! The first edit is always rigorous, and it's also where your book will improve the most. It may take your editor some time to get this first edit completed, especially if they also have other edits due during that time. Nothing could endear you to your publishing team more than patience.

Get in the right headspace to work with an editor

Stephen King gets edited. Toni Morrison got edited. George R.R. Martin gets edited (to some extent, anyway). The author of this book, who is an editor herself, needed an editor before publishing this book. It might hurt to hear, but your book was not born perfect, and you also need an editor. When you work so closely with your book for so long, you may start to lose sight of the trees for the forest. There are likely grammatical nuances or storytelling conventions you're not familiar with yet. Something might just sound weird, and you've never stopped to consider it before.

It's important to get in the right frame of mind to have your work edited by a professional, especially if you've never really been edited before. Being edited requires an author to swallow their pride, open their mind, and adopt a constructive, collaborative mindset. Much like co-parenting with the spouse you divorced, this process may be challenging, but it's what's best for your goblin child—sorry, your book.

Your editor is your partner. It's easy for an author to forget this while in the throes of an edit, but it's imperative that you remember this always. You and your editor are a team, and as a team, you share the single goal of creating the best book possible. You likely polished your book as best as you could before sending it off to seek publication; when your editor reads that version, they're imagining all that could be done to elevate that book to the next level. Both of these stages of manuscript are crucially important, much like how the author's and editor's perspectives are both crucially important.

When your editor sends your first edit and all you can see is criticism, remind yourself—this is critique, not criticism. The main difference between the two is intention. People criticize when they are feeling poorly and want the other person to feel just as poorly. People critique (hopefully consensually) when they want to help the other person improve. Your editor's only goal is to harness your book's full potential and maybe teach you a little something along the way.

As you go through your editor's notes, keep an open and collaborative mindset. Some of their recommendations will be grammatically necessary, while others will be stylistic. So while standing your ground about a specific comma your editor insists is grammatically inappropriate might not be a good use of your creative energy, you're absolutely welcome to disagree with your editor's stylistic notes, make a revision different from what they suggested, or explain yourself to give them more context. Outside of grammar, an editor's recommendations are just that: recommendations. An edit is a conversation between the writer and the editor, so it's important that you play your part.

Some of your editor's recommendations will in fact be grammatically necessary, however. Lots of writers have generally strong grammar skills, and plenty of authors will have their manuscripts edited by a friend or colleague before submitting. But it's important to remember that American publishers of fiction use a very specific grammar guide—*The Chicago Manual of Style*, to be exact. If you haven't seen a copy of this style guide, it's a vividly colored, near-thousand-page monolith of grammatical nuance and direction (now accessible and somehow longer online!). Your first instinct upon seeing this book might be to anxiously wonder, *How on Earth am I supposed to memorize all of that?!*

The answer is: you're not. That's your editor's job (to a certain extent). Those pages contain more grammatical roadmaps than any self-preserving person should ever seek to navigate. Searching for the answers to some of the more specific grammatical inquiries feels more like reading a "choose your own adventure" book. Often, there is a long list of if/then statements about which grammatical choices should be made under what circumstances. It's a veritable labyrinth, to be sure. But authors are not required nor even expected to navigate this labyrinth.

So get ready—and get excited—to be edited. Your book is going to change because it needs to. Don't resist the advice of your professional support. Keep an open mind, and find within your editor's notes the inspiration you need to get to editing.

Track Changes

You'll want to have a solid grasp on how to track changes in word processors before launching into a book publishing project. Microsoft Word and Apple Pages have Track Changes; Google Docs has "suggesting mode." As long as you're familiar with one of these programs, it shouldn't be hard for you to adapt to another.

When you're editing your book with an editor, every single change they make to your book (some structural formatting changes aside) will be using Track Changes. In return, you must do the same. It's crucially important that neither you nor your editor makes a change without the other person being able to see it. On the one hand, they may suggest a stylistic change that you know doesn't work with your book, and you need the opportunity to see it and comment on it; on the other hand, you may make some kind of change that is grammatically incorrect, and seeing it through Track Changes will bring your editor's attention to that section so they know they'll need to review it carefully.

The entire editing process happens through Track Changes and commenting. They are the language through which you can have this conversation with your editor. Take advantage of the tools you have at hand, and make sure you're comfortable using Track Changes before it's time to dive into an edit.

Developmental editing

Developmental editing is what it sounds like: your editor's notes about how you could develop your overall story. This doesn't involve line editing[19] (page 62) or copy editing[20] (page 63), though different kinds of editing may be done at the same time. When conducting a developmental edit, your editor will look for plot, character, consistency, and worldbuilding aspects that might be strengthened.

While line and copy editing happen right in your manuscript through Microsoft Word Track Changes or another tracking program, developmental editing might happen in an email. Some editors will write a letter containing a list of their developmental recommendations as well as note instances where those issues come up in the manuscript.

When you read your editor's most substantial notes in their first edit of your manuscript, your first impulse might be to get offended or defensive. You may even start to panic and feel some anxiety rising inside you. Not only is this reaction completely acceptable, it's also incredibly normal. Very few people enjoy being critiqued, and it can be really hard to hear outside opinions about the book, on which you are the biggest expert. Furthermore, you

19   line editing: *editing to review line-by-line language choices, complex grammar, and semantics*

20   copy editing: *editing very closely for spelling, grammar, and mechanics*

and your editor are only just starting out your relationship, and you may not fully trust them yet. This is okay.

Deny your urge to email back all of your first-impulse thoughts, no matter what those thoughts are. Thank your editor for their edit and then tell them you'll review their notes and get back to them. Give them a timeline for returning your first edit, if you think you have an idea of how long it might take you, or tell them you'll give them a timeline after you've had time to review all of their notes.

It's a good idea to review your editor's developmental notes in full, and then mull them over for a few days. If you feel they did not understand some fundamental aspect of your story, remember that they are not a warlock and cannot read your mind. They can only read what's on the page—much like your future readers. Let your editor's advice sit and process. If you're feeling injured, let those feelings wash over you. That kind of reaction is normal, but it's not helpful. Simmer your thoughts together with your editor's notes.

You may want to talk through some of your editor's bigger notes, and you deserve to! Often, your editor will seek to schedule a meeting with you after you've read through the first edit and before you begin enacting those edits and making some of your own changes to clear any confusion and talk through problem areas. Sometimes this conversation might be a simple email exchange. Go to your editor graciously, no matter your feelings about their edit. Talk about your thoughts—not your feelings—and work with them to come to an agreement about how problem areas will be addressed. At any such meeting, adopt the mindset that you and your editor are teammates who are trying to resolve the same issue. This attitude will help the collaboration and brainstorming flourish.

Then get to work! Enacting a developmental revision on your manuscript might seem daunting at first, but you can do it. View your editor's notes as a to-do list. The best way to tackle an overwhelming to-do list is to start with the smallest, easiest tasks so you can feel good about crossing stuff off. Do what comes easiest to you, cross it off, and then pick the next thing. (Don't forget to add "Write to-do list" at the top of your to-do list so when you finish writing the list you can cross that item off.)

This doesn't mean you are forced to simply accept all of your editor's notes, do as they've commanded, and shut up. No! This is a collaborative process, and your editor is relying on you to have a conversation with them through your edits. If your editor has made a recommendation you don't agree with, make a note to email them about it, or send an edit letter of your own along with your first edit back to them.

Your editor might make a recommendation that's simply wrong, because they don't understand your world as well as you do. For example, an editor might recommend you make it more clear that Taylor is in love with Alex. Whoops! You had actually intended for Taylor to be in love with Sam. You won't want to spend time making it clear that Taylor is in love with Alex; that's simply not correct in your story. Instead, ask your editor to help you find ways to reduce indicators that Taylor is in love with Alex and seek ways to reinforce that Taylor is in love with Sam.

Your editor might make a recommendation that will shift something big in your book. They might recommend you switch from third-person to first-person narration, or change the gender of a main character. They might recommend you cut the first couple of chapters so you can start with a stronger hook. You might think to yourself, *Well, that's impossible, because that's not how this story goes!* But ask yourself: Is there merit to what your editor is saying? What would really change if you took their recommendation? Would it truly upset the entire story? If so, would it possibly do more strengthening than destruction? Is there a way to compromise? What are your thoughts?

And some of your editor's notes—hopefully, fingers crossed—you'll read and say, "Brilliant! Why didn't I think of that?" And that is a beautiful feeling for everyone.

Here's what you're *not* going to do: ignore your editor's notes. It's okay to accidentally miss a few things and get to them on your next edit, but it's not okay to simply ignore your editor's notes because you disagree or find the work too hard. Editing is a team sport, and you can't let the team down. When you ignore your editor's notes—simply disregard the notes you don't like, do only the revisions you agree with, and send the manuscript back without trying to chat about these issues—you're sending your editor a clear message that you're not interested in doing your half of the work. We probably all know the old joke about group projects in school. Don't be that person who does nothing and still hopes to get the A.

Line editing

Line editing is this funny middle ground between large-scale developmental editing and small-scale copy editing, so it can sometimes be hard to define. For the most part, line editing focuses on the nuances of semantics, syntax, and linguistics, as well as clarity, authenticity, and voice. When line editing, your editor will be looking at your language use at the paragraph and sentence levels to try to smooth everything out, make your language sound pretty, and ensure all information is being conveyed in a straightforward manner.

A lot of the time, line editing is about cutting. A good editor loves to cut, and a good author lets them. Almost everyone says things in too many words almost all of the time. It's human nature, and it's super normal! But in a book, concision is often key. This isn't a composition class, and you don't need to meet a word count. When your editor recommends cutting some words—or many words—ask yourself if you really needed those words in the first place.

Your editor might make line edit revisions right in the text using Track Changes or similar, or they might make comments where they'd like to see a line revision. But it's not all hard work. Line editing can be the most fun part of the editing process. It's where the puzzle of language really comes into play, and the editor and author must work together to merge clarity with poetry, meaning with fluff, and voice with precision.

Copy editing

You know what's hard? Commas. You know what you don't have to fully understand to be a good writer? Commas. While you should certainly do your best to use good grammar, spelling, and mechanics in your manuscripts, these aspects of writing are so much less important for you to focus on than the story itself. A great editor can and should fix your grammatical errors for you, but they can't write your book for you.

The flip side of this is that you have to trust that your editor has a better understanding of grammar and mechanics than you. That's not a diss; it's just their job. We won't harp on this too much here; you can refer back to "Getting in the right headspace to work with an editor" (Page 54) if you're interested in further harping. Just know that your editor is very familiar with *The Chicago Manual of Style* and *Merriam-Webster's Dictionary*, and unless they make a silly mistake (It happens! Editors are human. That's why we proofread.), you should probably listen to what they have to say about grammar and mechanics.

For the most part, it's a good idea to just let the copy edit happen to you. You're in good hands. Your editor is doing the right thing. Ask questions if you want to learn, or don't if you don't. In the end, your book is going to sparkle!

Final thoughts about editing

Many editors perform some amount of developmental, line, and copy editing during each edit. In theory, most of the developmental editing will happen during the first edit, and by the final edit, they should be mostly copy editing. Your edits will look something like this:

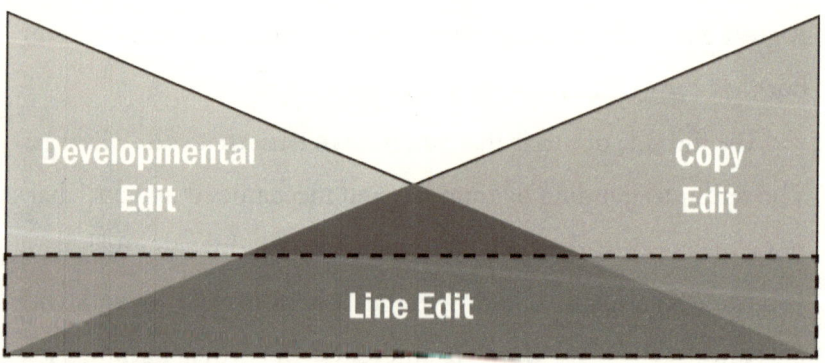

Each manuscript goes through two to four edits, occasionally more, each of which will likely be a blend of these levels of editing. Each edit will be less rigorous and more mechanical than the last. Upon completion of the final edit, both the editor and the author should feel really good about the shape the manuscript is in.

Proofread

Regardless of how confident the editor and author are about the manuscript, it will still go through a proofread. Your proofreader will be an editor who was not your primary editor. Their task is to catch glaring mechanical and spelling errors in this final editorial pass. They might weigh in on any issues you and your editor have not yet resolved.

The proofread is a very important step. You and your editor have been working on this project for so long that you are likely missing things. Your proofreader likely will not have read your manuscript before, so they'll be in the perfect position to note things you and your editor might have been missing all along.

Your project manager will send the proofread to you, and you'll get to respond to or enact those final changes. When you send your marked-up proofread back to your project manager, they'll go through and resolve and accept any remaining changes. When they're done, your manuscript should look clean and shiny and lovely with no lingering notes or Track Changes edits. They'll send you this version to use in seeking endorsements and other promotional endeavors.

This doesn't have to be the end of your text changes; it's totally possible to make small revisions to the text during design if you notice any lingering errors or funky language. However, your manuscript should be pretty much complete by the time the proofread is over. So while changes can be made during the design phase, we want to keep those changes as minimal as possible, and really only make changes that are necessary for grammar, consistency, or clarity.

Illustrations

Children's picture books, as their name suggests, feature illustrations. Some middle-grade or children's chapter books feature occasional illustrations, perhaps a couple throughout or at the start of each chapter. Some non-children's books may include illustrations as well. Some books may call for an illustrated cover but no illustrations inside. If you're not sure if your book should have illustrations, talk to your project manager.

It's worth mentioning again here that many—if not most—publishers give their authors little to no input on the illustration process. That's one of the negatives about traditional publishing we hope authors are aware of before they go into it. Traditionally publishing authors should be prepared to be left out of this process.

Getting ready for illustrations

When it's time to jump into the illustrations, your project manager will really take the lead, so it's important to let them drive and just hop in the car. They will reach out to the illustrator to make sure they're available, interested, and within budget. They will draft any necessary contracts—certainly one between the publisher and the illustrator, and possibly one between the publisher and author, if the author is investing any of the funds.

If you're self-publishing without a packager, you'll have to be your own project manager here. All of these steps, you'll have to do yourself, and you may need to lean on the illustrator of your choosing for their expertise, if they're amenable.

Laying out your book

At this point, your project manager will need to lay out your book. This won't be a nice, pretty, professional book layout—that will come later, when your illustrations are done and the designer gets their hands on it. Probably using Post-Its, your project manager will lay out where your text and illustrations should go so they can figure out how many illustrations you'll need in what sizes to make the book the right length.

Your project manager will use this layout to determine what kinds of illustrations your book will need, and how many in each size. Here are some of the different kinds of illustrations:

Spot illustrations

Spot illustrations are small illustrations that typically only feature one or two characters or items and little to no background. If you're illustrating your book on a tight budget, your project manager may choose to use many spot illustrations to get more bang for your buck.

Vignette illustrations

Vignette illustrations typically feature a small scene with a couple of characters and a limited background. These illustrations do not reach the edges of the page, but instead have faded or shaped edges.

Half-page illustrations

Half-page illustrations are similar to vignettes in that they typically feature just a couple characters and a simple background. The main difference is that vignette illustrations tend to have faded edges that are not designed to reach the edges of the page, whereas half-page illustrations are designed to go all the way to the edge of a page on three of its sides. A vignette is like a complex spot illustration, whereas a half-page illustration is like a one-page illustration chopped right in half.

One-page illustrations

One-page illustrations take up the entirety of one single page of a book from top to bottom, from crease to edge. Your project manager may choose to put text on the page opposite from a one-page illustration, or they may choose to ask your illustrator to reserve a certain amount of space for text somewhere on the one-page illustration.

Two-page illustrations (next page)

Two-page illustrations (also called "two-page spreads" because they *spread* across two pages) cover the entirety of two facing pages of a book, from top to bottom, across the center crease. Your project manager will likely ask the illustrator to reserve space for text somewhere on the two-page spread.

art by Zach Urtes

Art direction

Your illustrator will be a professional artist, so they'll be able to make choices regarding color, scale, layout, etc. However, they need to know the important details of your story so they can make sure the illustrations capture everything you want them to. Sometimes, your project manager may choose to send the illustrator a copy of your manuscript so they can get the full picture. Whether or not the illustrator reads the manuscript, you will definitely need to send clear and concise illustration descriptions.

Character description(s)

Write down your vision for your main character(s). This should include things like the character's age (or approximate age), gender, ethnicity, hair color and type, and outfit (if relevant). This may also include other important details like physical ability (a wheelchair, glasses, a prosthetic arm), crucial accessories (like Harriet the Spy's notebook she's never without), and time period (if not contemporary).

Illustration descriptions

There are lots of different ways to go about developing illustration descriptions, so be sure to listen to your project manager's guidance here. Generally, you or your project manager will write a short description of your vision for each illustration. Write down the things that are really important—non-negotiables—and let the illustrator do the rest. That's their job!

You'll definitely want to include what characters are in each illustration, where they're located, and what they're doing. You may also want to include facial expressions and body language. Even if it seems obvious in the text, spell it out.

Be real with yourself about what is important in your illustration descriptions. The color of someone's shirt or the exact kind of tree in your illustration is probably not important. (If your book is called *Carlos and the Purple Sweatshirt*, then I stand corrected.) The fact that you'd "really like" for the main character to look just like your daughter is sweet, but is it crucial? If the illustrator tells you that the curly-haired protagonist isn't working against the ivy wall background, why fight it?

However, there are some instances in which you'll want to provide a lot of detail in your illustration descriptions and even possibly reference pictures. For example, if your book is historical (fiction or nonfiction), you'll want the illustrations to be historically accurate. You may want to include reference pictures for how people back then dressed or what their houses looked like.

You'll also want to be extremely specific in your descriptions and possibly include reference pictures if your illustrations depict something super specific, like a certain kind of computer or species of flower. If your book talks about specific cultural objects or rituals, you'll want to describe those thoroughly as well.

In summary, give your illustrator exactly as much information as they need to sketch your vision correctly, and nothing more. They're the visual experts here, and they'll take your descriptions and turn them into something awesome!

Finding the right illustrator

The hardest part of the illustration process is finding the right illustrator. There is a ton of great talent out there, so the search for your book can feel overwhelming at first. Your project manager will help you find the right illustrator for your project based on a lot of factors, including the following:

Budget

There is an incredible range in what an illustrator may charge for their work. Illustrating a whole book can start at around a thousand dollars, and the high end of the price range is probably infinity. Some of the more affordable illustrators create amazingly beautiful work, while some of the super expensive options might not be your style at all.

Are you paying for your illustrations, or is your publisher? Is your publisher willing to invest up to a certain amount, and any balance will be up to you to fund? If you're not sure, chat with your project manager to get a better idea of what their expectations are for budgeting your book's illustrations.

Timeline

This might sound obvious to some people, but it'll be news to others: illustrations are art, and art takes time. Some illustrators can get a lot of work done quickly, while others might need an extended timeline. Some illustrators may not be able to start your project right now, but they could start in a month or two after they've wrapped up their current projects. Ask

yourself if you're willing to wait for the right illustrator or if you'd rather find someone who can get illustrations done in a timely manner.

Style

There are as many styles of illustrations as there are illustrators—or probably more, since many illustrators are so skilled

FUN FACT

Some illustrators may try to tell you that they don't work under deadlines. No, that's not a joke. Illustrators who can't work under any deadlines are not professionals, and you should steer clear of them. With no mutually agreed upon deadlines, how are you supposed to enforce that they get the work done at all?

that they can switch between styles. There are technical terms that can describe these styles, but you don't need to know them. Your project manager will take the lead on illustrations, so let them! They have experience working with illustrators, using the right language to communicate with illustrators, and making sure the illustrations are done in such a way that the final book will look amazing.

The best way to home in on the style you want your book's illustrations to have is to look through other illustrated books and note the ones you like. Take a walk through your local indie bookstore and pick up some books whose styles speak to you. Share the books and illustrators you like with your project manager. They'll use your preferences to find the right illustrator for you.

Don't forget to take your project manager's advice here as well. The fact that you really like a certain style of illustration doesn't mean it's the right look for your project. If your book is contemporary and energetic, classic watercolor illustrations aren't the right look. If your book has a very classic feel, maybe watercolors are appropriate. Take your project manager's input seriously.

Have we mentioned that you should listen to your project manager?

Medium

Speaking of watercolors—let's talk about medium. Not "I'll have a medium fries, thanks." The medium of your illustrations means the kind of art supplies that are used to create them, whether that be paint (oil, watercolor, acrylic, etc.), pencil (colored or grayscale), digital, or otherwise. These media give different vibes to your book, but they also have different pros and cons that might arise in the illustration process.

Traditional art

Traditionally in history, computers didn't exist, and therefore "traditional" art is that which is not made using a computer. Traditional art means the illustrator is creating this artwork in the real world by hand on a piece of paper or a canvas. More classic art media like watercolor can be extremely idyllic and beautiful, which is why many people appreciate it. However, watercolor is relatively final. Once the illustrator has put paintbrush to paper, that color is there for good. There is no eraser for watercolor, and any revisions must be made based on what is there. A watercolor artist simply cannot make the blue ball red (but they might be able to make it purple by adding red!). That means that revisions can be quite challenging. If you have a correction to an illustration—and most books' illustration processes do involve some corrections—a watercolor artist may have to start over entirely to make that one change.

Traditional art presents some other obstacles, like digitization. While digital art (below) is art that is created digitally on a computer or other device, any book illustration must at some point be digitalized so it can be included in the book, which is designed digitally. If your illustrator paints a giant watercolor for your book cover, how are we going to get that onto a computer? Photos of illustrations rarely translate the colors correctly, and most scanners are 11x17". Your illustrator is going to have to track down an oversized, professional-grade scanner at some office store or similar, and that kind of specialized scanning will cost extra. Beyond the size difference, professional scanners at print and office shops are simply much better quality for scanning vivid illustrations than home scanners that are primarily designed to scan documents.

Digital art

Digital art is art that the illustrator has created on their computer or other electronic device. Digital art can be quite varied, as there are as many options in a digital art program as a person can imagine. The best thing about digital art, however, is how easy it is to make revisions. If watercolor paintings are a printed book, only capable of changing in major ways if you simply start from scratch and try again, then digital art is your Google Doc, simple to change and share.

For the most part these days, for the reasons listed above, digital art is the vastly preferred way of getting a book illustrated. Any style of traditional art can be replicated by the right digital artist.

Digital art is often much less expensive for the illustrator to produce, as they simply have to pay the recurring fees for their programs rather than constantly replenishing paint, pencils, and other supplies. These kinds of savings on the illustrators' part can lead to better pricing for the author and publisher.

The fact that traditional art is so hard to make corrections to is a serious consequence of choosing that type of media. Digital art can be changed with a few clicks of a button. Art programs make it so easy for illustrators to try different things to see what works best, undo something they didn't end up liking, or change color palettes. Your illustrations are almost certainly going to need revisions, and you want those to go as smoothly as possible.

Final thoughts about illustration medium

Talk to your project manager about what art media might be best for your book project. Odds are they're going to recommend digital. But if you feel strongly about using a certain traditional medium, let your project manager know, and explain your reasoning to them. Together, you'll figure out the right approach for your book.

References

Before you start working with a plumber or therapist (or book publisher), you're going to want to check out their references to make sure other people have had good experiences with them. Your book's illustrator is no different. You'll want to do your best to learn what you can about any illustrator before you reach out to them about illustrating your book.

Digital versus Traditional Media

	Pros	**Cons**
Digital media	• Revisions are simpler to enact. • Illustrations are already digitized. • Illustrators can easily provide options for the author to choose from.	• Digital illustrations tend to look more immature and may not be appropriate for more mature work.
Traditional media	• Classic feel • The author may be able to hold onto the original art as a keepsake (though be sure to discuss this ahead of time!).	• Revisions are a huge pain, and illustrations may even need to be redone entirely to enact a revision. • Can be a challenge to digitize • Stylistically often feels older, less modern

However, most illustrators won't have a list of references on their website for you to hop on the horn and get in touch with. So where should you look?

Their agency or company

Some illustrators are represented by an agency or work through some other kind of company. If that's true, you may be required to work through that organization to contract with their illustrator rather than with the individual themself. An illustrator who works through an organization is often a highly skilled, highly professional artist who does this for a living. In these cases, the agency will often ensure that the illustrator is getting the work done correctly and on deadline. If you want further information about working with said illustrator, there may be references on the organization's website, or you may be able to request them.

Online Reviews

Check out the illustrator's social media if you can find them there! While Instagram may not tell you anything about the illustrator other than that their work is pretty, Facebook has a whole "Reviews" tab for professional pages where people may have left reviews of their work with the illustrator.

Depending on how popular the illustrator is, they may have Google reviews as well. Google reviews are usually only available to businesses, so for your illustrator to have Google reviews, they will have to be operating through or as a business. This means that they're either working through an agency or similar, as we mentioned above, or they have a business, like an LLC, for their art. Google reviews for an illustrator's agency will be for the organization as a whole, but if you read through them, you may be able to find specific mentions of the illustrator you're interested in working with.

Just ask

If getting reviews is really important to you and you're not finding what you want by searching around online, it's okay to request that your project manager ask the illustrator if they have any references.

The illustration process

Illustrator contract

If you're working with a project manager, they will likely handle the entire illustration process for you, including writing a contract for the illustrator. But if you're hiring your own illustrator, it's a good idea to get them to sign a contract.

For those who don't have experience with contracts, the mere notion of writing and enforcing a contract can seem daunting. Some contracts really do seem like they're written in another language understood only by lawyers and landlords. But a contract is merely a written agreement between two or more parties, and they do *not* have to be so complicated that no one can understand them.

Most contracts should include the names of the parties involved, along with what those parties are responsible for. In this case, the two parties would be the author, who is responsible for payment and feedback, and the illustrator, who is responsible for producing art and enacting feedback. Contracts should include specific numbers, like how many illustrations in what sizes are being requested for what dollar amount. Dates and timelines are important as well, like when payment will be rendered and when the work should be completed. A contract should also have some kind of termination agreement that explains under what circumstances either party would be permitted to end this agreement and what each party would need to do after termination (like paying balances or providing draft files).

For these kinds of basic contracts, you can run a simple Google search for templates, cut what you don't need, and plug in your own information. However you write your contract, don't forget the most important part: both parties must sign!

What to send your illustrator

I can't emphasize enough that if you're working with a project manager, they will do all of this for you, and you should probably just let them do it. If you're not working with a project manager, here's what you can consider sending to your illustrator to get them started.

<u>Character descriptions</u>

You wrote them; they need them. You can send your character descriptions first, while you're still working on your illustration descriptions. You can also send everything at once, though, and request the illustrator do the character sketch(es) first. You definitely want to make sure everyone is on the same page about characters before the illustrator puts them in fifteen different bigger illustrations, which will be harder to change than just the sketch. However, it's important to remember that while you are passionate about your book, everyone else who works on it is doing just that—working. Your illustrator may not have time to read your manuscript, or they might just not care to. That's okay! You don't need them to fall in love with your book; you just need them to illustrate it beautifully.

Illustration descriptions

I mean, yeah, your illustrator is going to need those illustration descriptions! Send them your descriptions along with any additional context they may need.

Reference photos

If your illustrations are going to include real people, real settings, unique cultural objects or settings, important scientific equipment, or other specific details, it's a good idea to send reference pictures. Your illustrator may be able to Google the subject matter, but their search may yield results that show the setting from a different angle, or the artifact from a different time period, or the character at a different age from what you'd intended.

The manuscript

Giving the illustrator the opportunity to read the manuscript they're illustrating can help inform them about its tone and themes, which they can then imbue in the illustrations. Children's picture books can be read in a few minutes, and illustrators can quickly and easily increase their understanding of their task this way. If an artist is illustrating a cover or chapter header images for a chapter book, it's a bigger request to ask they read the book in full, but you can always send it and let them read it if they want to.

Sketches

Sketches are a great way to make sure that you, your project manager, and your illustrator are all on the same page before the illustrator adds color to your illustrations.

Character sketches

The character and illustration descriptions go to the illustrator, who, as is mentioned on the previous page, will likely start with a character sketch. The purpose of the character sketch is to make sure the author, illustrator, and project manager are all on the same page. Once the character sketch has been approved, the illustrator will go on to sketch all the illustrations.

Illustration sketches

Your illustrator will start by sketching out their interpretations of your illustration descriptions, which they'll send to your project manager for approval. The sketch phase is where all non-color illustration corrections need to take place. Notes on color can wait for the illustrations to be rendered in color later; for now, it's important to bring up any issues regarding shape, size, spacing, and other basic illustration features.

If you or your project manager request any changes, the illustrator will provide updated sketches. You may go back and forth like this several times before the sketches suit your book's needs and are ready to go to color.

Final illustrations

Once the sketches are approved, the illustrator will go on to color and otherwise finalize the illustrations. The only corrections that should be taking place at this time pertain to color and some high-definition details that may not have been apparent in the sketches.

Once all final illustrations have been approved, the illustrator will provide official, final, high-resolution illustration files, and their balance will be paid.

Endorsements

Endorsements are book reviews authors receive before their book is complete for the purpose of putting them on the cover or an interior page of the book itself. Endorsements can also show up in online retail and review sites. Endorsements can encourage someone who is looking at your book online or in the store to purchase it; they help create emotion and prestige around your book before a reader has opened it. It would be a little braggadocious for an author or publisher to say, "An absolutely stunning book that sparkles like a miracle," or "Shocking ending that will stick with you long after you read," or "Un-put-downable!" on their own book. But if someone else says it, it's a great compliment!

Who should endorse?

This is a great question with a complicated answer. It's a good idea to seek endorsements from experts in the subject matter of your book. That way, their opinion about your book will carry some weight. (It's great if your property manager loves your book, but really, unless the book is about property management, what do they know?) It's possible that someone who is considering reading your book will recognize this subject matter expert or their work and make the choice to purchase your book exclusively because of that. Even to someone who doesn't recognize the endorser or their work, the mere fact of someone in a position of authority recommending your book may be very influential!

Answers to the question of who is a subject matter expert can vary a lot. If your book is a nonfiction piece about dinosaurs, it's pretty simple to search for other dinosaur experts, like archaeologists or paleontologists. Some subjects allow you to cast a broader net for relevant endorsers. If you've written a book about parenting, you could reach out to teachers, school counselors, youth therapists, childcare experts, or even parenting bloggers.

If your book is a novel, good endorsers might be other authors who write in the same genre. If you write romantic comedies, try to find another author who writes rom coms—ideally, someone who has a substantial following. If you write fantasy, finding another fantasy author would be ideal, but you would probably also find value in an endorsement from a contemporary fiction or science fiction author as well.

Endorsements carry a bit less sway for children's books. When it comes to children's books, it's important to remember that the person purchasing is not the reader, but their adult guardian. Getting endorsements from teachers or librarians would put in a great word to parents that your book is educational or at least educator-approved. For some children's books about certain topics, like anxiety or grief, psychologists who specialize in your subject matter or target age group would make good endorsers.

Write down a list of potential endorsers. Don't worry about listing too many people; any number may say no, if they answer at all. If you end up getting more endorsements than you can fit on the front and/or back covers, you can put some on the interior of the book, on your book's online listings, or on your website. It's a good idea to note some "shoot for the stars" potential endorsers along with some "sure bet" endorsers.

Shoot for the stars

You can shoot for the stars by reaching out to celebrities, popular social media influencers, or other thought leaders in your subject matter. The world's leading dinosaur expert or a popular archaeological TikToker would be good examples of "shoot for the stars" options for your dinosaur book. For your novel, "shoot for the stars" might mean reaching out to famous or semi-famous authors or those with excellent social media followings.

What makes a "popular" social media influencer? There's no hard and fast rule, but when comparing all social accounts, an influencer with at least tens of thousands of followers could be considered fairly popular.

"Shoot for the stars" does not apply to Oprah, Dolly Parton, the president, or Jon Krakauer. These people are what we call "superstars." Not only do they probably not have time to even consider the thousands of requests people would like to send them; they likely cannot even be reached. Celebrities go to great lengths to avoid being contacted. If you want Katie Couric to endorse your book, you better have dated her in high school. Otherwise, it ain't happening.

Get some sure bets

Also include in your list some "sure bets." These are people who are easily contacted and likely to be willing. Often, these sure bets are people you already know or have at least interacted with on social media. Other authors in your area would be good for this part of your list, or people you personally know through your subject matter. For example, if you're a teacher who wrote a kids' book, you can ask other teachers you know or even your school's principal for an endorsement.

Choosing who to ask for endorsements is a matter of who you know versus who you wish you knew. Star shooting and sure betting are both important here. Shooting for the stars can really elevate your book if it pays off, but you need to maintain the mentality that it's possible that none of them will respond to you. That's where the sure bets come in.

How to find endorsers' contact information

If you're seeking an endorsement from a colleague, a friend, or someone you've already connected with on social media, just shoot them a request in the way you normally communicate. Email them, text them, or send them a personal message on social media. You can also call to request an endorsement, but you'll definitely want to email them the details later if they agree verbally over the phone.

If you're reaching out to someone you don't know, try your hardest to find an email address for them. Check their social media bios; sometimes people who are really keen to be contacted will put their emails there. If not, they might have their website listed, or a Linktree that will lead you to their website or email address. If this person is quite famous, you might find contact information for their agent or manager instead, which is a great place to start trying to track them down.

If you can't find an email address, the next step would be to try to message them on social media. Most social media platforms have direct messaging. Sometimes, bigger celebrities turn off that direct messaging feature so random people (sorry, that's you) can't reach out to them. A lot of the time, bigger celebrities or online personalities have the direct message feature but never check or respond to their messages. This is all normal, and you must respect people's right to privacy. If it's clear they've made every effort to avoid being contacted, don't contact them.

How to request an endorsement

If you find this person's email address, congrats! That's half the battle. Shoot them a short email—repeat: *short*—featuring the crucial information. Say hello, tell them you like their work (being as specific as possible), and then ask if they'd be willing to write an endorsement of your book. Be sure to include:

- your book's genre
- your book's synopsis
- your book's word count
- your book's age range (or middle grade, YA, adult)
- the deadline by which you would like the endorsement returned

Be sure to tell any endorser you will use their endorsement "in or on the book." You might think you want to put a certain endorser's endorsement right on the front cover. But what if they surprise you by writing a kind of lame endorsement? You don't want to promise anything before you know what you're working with.

If you haven't found an email address and you need to write a direct message instead, you'll want to use the same approach but make it even shorter. You could even just start by asking "Hi! Love your work on X. Do you write endorsements for books?" The longer a direct social media message is, the less likely it is to be read.

The goal with a direct message is to move the conversation to email as soon as possible. If this person expresses interest, ask for their email address so you can send them more information. Then circle back to the beginning of this section and follow the email instructions. Even if you've already told them the basic facts about your book in the direct message, you'll still want to list them again in the email just so they have everything in one place.

It's important to focus on one line item from the list of details above: the deadline you need this endorsement by. Time works in mysterious ways, and it doesn't move at the same pace for everyone. You might be surprised how many people would take six months or more to get an endorsement done and not think twice about it—or let it fall off their radar entirely. Speak with your project manager before you send anything to anyone to make sure you both agree on a deadline for endorsements. You don't want your book's production to come to a halt because you're waiting for someone else.

If you send an email and don't hear back for a couple of weeks, follow up once, "just confirming you received this email." If you don't hear back on that follow-up, move on. There's not much point in following up on a direct message; either they read it or they didn't, and either they're interested or they're not. Unfortunately, a lot of people simply won't respond if they're not interested. Never put all your eggs in one basket; never hold out for one endorser who hasn't yet expressed interest at the cost of your book's production timeline.

What to send to your endorser

Consult your project manager to figure out how to send your manuscript to your endorsers. If the book is not yet designed, you can send a PDF of your manuscript file. If it's in design, you can send the in-progress design file. Just be sure to, no matter what, tell your endorser that you are sending them an "uncorrected" version of your book. They're welcome to bring errors to your attention, but they need to know that if they see something wonky, it's going to be fixed, and it should not affect their opinion of your book. A Word file can be called an "uncorrected manuscript;" a PDF design file can be called an "uncorrected galley."[21]

Vetting endorsements

When you get an endorsement back from an endorser, it will be great, lackluster, or just plain mystifying. It's easy to head this off by being specific about what you're looking for and sending

21   *uncorrected galley: a version of your book that is in the design process but not yet complete*

your endorser examples of endorsements you like. But you might still get something funky in return. These people are doing you a favor, so it can be a delicate dance if you don't receive the kind of endorsement you thought you would. Here are some tips for navigating the land of endorsements.

Most of them will be great, and that's great. If your endorser sends you a great endorsement—one that is well-written, specific to your book, and complimentary—thank the endorser emphatically. After all, they've just done you a wonderful favor. Forward the endorsement to your project manager, who will proofread it for errors, or if you're self-publishing, proofread it yourself and save it for later in design.

Some endorsements can be kind of bad. They probably won't say something bad about your book—the odds are good that an endorser who doesn't like your book will simply decline to endorse it. However, some endorsements are merely uninspired regurgitations of your synopsis. They may just not sparkle! "This was a good read and really enjoyable." Ugh. Lame. It doesn't tell you anything about this book at all!

So what do you do? Start by thanking the endorser. Even if their endorsement isn't working for you, they've still given you their time and energy, so always thank them. Then you could ask the endorser to try to write another version of their endorsement, maybe one that focuses more on the vibe of the book than its plot, if they've merely written a synopsis. Remind them that the synopsis will be on the back cover of the book. Ask them if they could please revise their endorsement to include specific elements of your book. In short, don't be afraid to ask them to try again.

If the person who wrote you a sort of lame endorsement is a famous author or another big name, maybe it doesn't even matter that the endorsement doesn't sparkle; it's enough that it exists. If you manage to pull an endorsement from a well-loved author, their name on your book will say it all. Besides that, they likely don't have time to rewrite their endorsement anyway. You might want to just hang onto whatever that famous person wrote for you and be grateful you have it.

Some endorsements can be really befuddling to read. Some endorsers, especially those who have never sought or been asked to write an endorsement before, may have no idea what to do and will send you something you didn't expect. Some endorsements come back looking like train-of-consciousness reactions, like, "I LOVED this dang book so much I cannot BELIEVE IT!!!! Like seriously I would give it to everyone five stars. And can you believe the characters? Like LITERALLY SO SEXY!" This is a really silly example . . . until you get an endorsement that looks like this.

Ask yourself how valuable this endorsement is to you. If this is the only endorsement you're getting, you want it to be solid. You want it to look professional, be easy to read, and inspire others to pick up your book. In that case, you could ask for a rewrite. You could also harness this energy into a proper endorsement and send it back to the endorser, asking if they approve of your revisions. (You can always blame your publisher for not accepting the original! Unless you're self-publishing.)

If this is one of fifteen endorsements you're getting and the author isn't a well-known name, maybe just take the loss and thank them for their time. The endorsement can go on the interior of your book where people won't see it as easily, or you could even keep it off your book entirely and use it on your website.

If an endorsement is really that bad, and you can't figure out a good path to getting a better one, just thank the endorser and let the endorsement die in your inbox. Protect your book at all costs. Don't put something bonkers on your book just because you feel like you have to.

And for the love of all that is good and bookish, consult your project manager about all of this. A skilled project manager will be able to help you draft the language you need to get that elevated endorsement; they'll be able to rearrange that bananas endorsement so it shines; they'll be the bad guy who said the endorser needs to rewrite their endorsement or it can't go in the book.

Design

The design phase of any book's production is extremely exciting and validating for everyone who has been working on it thus far. Design is when your Word file becomes a proper book; the text gets laid out, and the cover comes to life. For lack of better phrasing, this is when a manuscript becomes a "real book."

Because the design phase is so important and special, the most important quality an author can have during this time is patience. While each project manager has ten or twenty projects on their plate at once, and each author only has one, the design team is responsible for the assembly of every single book a publisher ever produces, including both the books the publisher is producing under their imprint and any self-publishing projects. The design team is likely also working on things like social media graphics, e-book conversions, and all the other pretty little things that help a book sell. Any book or graphic design is also an artistic process, which can take time! The worst thing to do is rush the designer and end up with a cover or layout that no one is happy with.

Design elements

Your designer and your project manager will work together to make certain choices about your book's design. Most of these will be non-negotiable, as they'll depend on your book's stats, genre, and other details.

If you're self-publishing, it's a good idea to do some research about these elements to make the most informed decisions for your book.

This is not a time to be jazzy and creative for no reason. If you produce a book outside of its genre standards, people will notice, and they may be put off by those seemingly odd choices. It's better to choose the recommended options for your genre and let your creativity show in other ways.

Format(s)

Your book will be available in one or more formats, which may include casebound hardcover (no dust jacket), hardcover with dust jacket, paperback, e-book, and audiobook. Some books come out in hardcover first and then the paperback is released later. Some books are only produced in paperback (an affordable choice for publisher and reader). Some publishers will produce audiobooks for certain titles; some publishers may not do audiobooks or may choose not to produce one for your book.

Just about every book these days is and should be available as an e-book. With digital book sales at unprecedented heights, you would be doing yourself and your book a disservice opting not to produce an e-book. It takes little time and effort to convert a book into an e-book, so be sure you're getting one.

Trim size

Your trim size is the dimensions of your book in inches (not including the spine depth). The spine depth is determined by the number of pages. Your trim size is basically how big your cover is. For example, the book in your hands (assuming you've bought the print copy) is six inches across and nine inches tall, so its trim size is 6x9".

Generally, children's books are larger. A children's book might be an 8.5x8.5" square or a 7x10" rectangle. Square books are generally for younger kids; the rectangle books are generally for older kids who are working on transitioning to chapter books.

Most fiction is published at 5x8" or 5.5x8.5", though there is some variation. Most nonfiction is published at 6x9" or so, though again, there is some variation.

Cover finish

Covers are either glossy (shiny) or matte (not shiny). The book in your hands (assuming you've bought the print copy) is glossy. Glossy covers are great for children's picture books, as the glossy covering makes the books more durable. You can literally use a wet wipe to clean a glossy cover.

Matte covers are typically reserved for books designated for older audiences. However, this isn't a rule, and there are many glossy covers on adult and YA books. Other factors, like your cover design and coloring, may influence your designer or project manager to choose one over the other. For example, if your cover features a dark night sky, you wouldn't want a glossy cover, as that would catch a glare of any nearby lights or the sun and brighten that sky on your cover.

It's worth noting that glossy covers are reflective and therefore challenging to photograph. Matte covers won't betray the reflection of your phone in your hand taking a picture.

Paper

Your designer will determine the color and weight of the paper your book's interior will be printed on. Generally, the only color options will be white or crème. Often, crème is the better choice, as white paper with black text can seem very clinical. White paper is a great option for textbooks and other formal, scholarly writing. It's also a good option for children's picture books, so the color illustrations will print accurately. For most other books, crème is the move.

Your paper weight will depend on your genre. Children's picture books are printed on thicker, more durable paper (50#) that can withstand both young grabbing hands and the heaps of ink needed to print the vivid illustrations. Same with photo books, graphic novels, and other books that heavily feature images. Novels and the rest are typically printed on lighter paper (70#).

Interior design

The designer will lay out the interior of your book per the *Chicago Manual of Style* guidelines on how a book is structured, along with the printer's specifications.

The Parts of a Book

(adapted and abridged from *The Chicago Manual of Style*)

- Front matter

  - Title page(s)

    - Half title (optional)

    - Series title or frontispiece (optional)

    - Title page

  - Copyright page

  - Dedication and/or epigraph (optional)

  - Table of contents (optional)

  - Front matter text

    - Acknowledgments (optional)

    - Foreword, preface, and/or introduction (optional)

  - Other Front Matter

    - List of abbreviations (optional)

    - Publisher's, translator's, and editor's notes (optional)

    - List of illustrations or tables (if applicable)

- Text

  - Text subdivisions

- Back Matter

  - Acknowledgments, if they're not featured in the front matter (optional)

  - Appendixes, glossary, endnotes, and/or index (if applicable)

- Bibliography or reference list (if applicable)
- About the author
- About the illustrator (if applicable)

Picture book interiors

Designing the interior of a children's picture book primarily involves the marrying of the text to the illustrations. Your designer will have to fit the text and illustrations of your book together like a puzzle, with some help from the tentative layout that your project manager developed before you started illustrations. Children's picture books are often designed to be bold and bright with easy-to-read text.

Non-picture book interiors

For non-picture books—chapter books—"adult books," if you will, though not like *that*—the interior design will focus more on text treatment, formatting, and flourishes. Your designer will choose a font that's appropriate for your subject matter and target audience and lay out your book page by page. They'll design chapter headings and find the right symbol to use in section breaks, if those appear in your book.

Your designer may choose to start by creating an interior template that features the first chapter or so of your book. That way you can take a look at their vision for your book's interior and make any comments before they lay out the whole thing.

Cover design

This is probably the most fun and most important step of the entire book production process. People say, "Don't judge a book by its cover," but this expression applies to just about everything *except* book covers. An attention-grabbing cover can make or break a sale, so excellence is key here.

Your designer will likely not have read your book. This is just a reality of the industry. If a designer is designing thirty books per year (average for a fairly small independent press), they simply do not have time to read all of those, and especially not *before* they start on the design. (They can buy your book later based on its pretty cover and get to it when they can.) That's where your project manager comes in. Your project manager will have read your book in full—likely several times—by the time it gets to the design phase. They will have a conversation (or a few) with your designer about the book's tone, subject matter, and target audience, along with any notes they have from you, to give the designer a good idea of where to start.

Not everyone has a knack for color, shape, layout—art! Not everyone is an artist. Your job here is to be the author. Your designer's job is to be the artist and make the best cover possible for your book. Listen to your designer and your project manager when the time comes to design your book's cover. They know the industry better than you, they've had more training than you, and they know what works.

However, here's one important distinction to keep in mind.

While your designer is an *artist*, a graphic design artist, they are not an *illustrator*. Your designer will be able to use stock imagery, text treatments, abstract shapes and colors, and other people's illustrations to produce your book.

If you request a young brunette girl riding a horse into the sunset, your designer will look for a stock image featuring those elements. The more specific the request, the less likely they are to find exactly what you're looking for. It may be better to hire a photographer and shoot your own photo if it's so important to be incredibly specific—though a photoshoot is a huge financial and creative investment.

If you want a specific scene from your book depicted on the cover, an illustration may be in order. That will cost additional time and money from the author, the publisher, or both. An illustrated cover would be more appropriate for a YA cover than, say, a non-fiction cover. But there are always exceptions.

Get with your project manager if you're unsure what the game-plan for your cover is. They'll be able to advise you about all this and more.

Picture book covers

Children's picture book covers often come from the reuse of an interior illustration, amped up and stylized for a cover by the designer. This is a very common, cost-effective way of achieving a fun, appropriate cover. Alternatively, authors or publishers may wish to invest in a cover illustration separate from the interior illustrations, which can be fun (and expensive)!

Middle-grade and young adult covers

Middle-grade and young adult book covers in particular need to be extremely hip and grab the reader's attention right away. Your designer will likely put together a cover that's sharp, sleek, colorful, and fun to get those younger readers' attention. While these kinds of books are often not illustrated inside, they can totally benefit from an illustrated cover. This is a great idea to chat about with your project manager.

Fiction covers

Fiction covers, especially for adults, may be more abstract and artistic. With a little guidance, the designer is highly skilled in bringing text, images, colors, and patterns together to create a cohesive cover. Often, a fiction cover will convey the vibe of a book rather than something specific about the content of the book. For certain genres, an illustrated cover might also be appropriate for adult fiction.

Memoir and nonfiction covers

Memoirs and nonfiction titles may benefit from having a photograph or other memento on the front cover! This is a great way to grab a reader's attention while also alluding to the subject matter of the book. Any photos provided for the front cover will need to be high-resolution images, and your designer or project manager can advise about those specifications. Photos that are low-resolution, like an old family photo, for example, are not ideal for covers and run the risk of printing pixelated.

Pricing

Cover prices are the bane of the indie publishing world. The Big Five can afford to print thousands of copies of all their books offset (learn more about offset printing on Page 128), and by printing in bulk, their cost per copy lowers drastically. They can sell four-hundred-page paperbacks for under ten dollars and still make a profit due to sheer volume.

Independent publishers can't do this. They don't have the funds to print thousands of copies all at once, especially not an author's debut book. They don't have the resources to distribute all of those books. They don't have the sheer volume, the sheer brute sales force of the Big Five. This is a great example of why monopolies are bad for the small folk just doing their best to make some special art.

If you're publishing your book through an independent book publisher, the odds are good that your cover price might seem higher than you're used to. The prices they assign to their books are a result of the printer's prices.

A printer charges a certain amount per copy to print a book. The number on the cover is the cover price. The cover price minus the wholesale discount and printer fees is the net profit. That net profit gets split in two, with part of it staying with the publisher and part of it going to the author as royalties (learn more about royalties on Page 35). Both the publisher and the author have their own expenses that must come out of this figure. With all of these factors in mind, it's easy to see why a book's cover price is so important—and why it's so frustrating for indie publishers that the Big Five get to set the bar in the industry.

Be gentle with your publisher. They will assign you the best cover price they can that still leaves both parties a chance at making a profit.

Final thoughts about covers

There are a ton of different paths to creating an excellent cover. Your designer and project manager will work together to guide your cover's development. In the end, you'll have a cover that you love that will also intrigue potential buyers in person and online.

Miscellaneous design elements

There are other small, random design elements your book will need, and you may or may not have to be a part of the process of obtaining or producing them.

Author photo

It's common to end a book with a page featuring a photo of the author(s) (and illustrator, if there is one) along with a short biography about them. Your project manager might ask for these items at any point in the production process, and your designer may install them in your book at any point in the design process. But if they're not already handled by the end of design, they need to get done ASAP.

Your author photo will often be a nice, professional headshot or close body shot photograph of you. It's not recommended to include other people in the photo (unless you're working with a co-author or happen to know the illustrator in real life). These photos are not usually candids, though a strong candid could work.

It's important to have a good photo of yourself. The light should be coming from in front of you or to your side, not from behind you. The background should be simple, either a solid color or unobtrusive pattern. Bricks are nice if you're in a city; trees are nice if you're in the country. A solid-colored wall is a great option too.

You should be dressed. Yes. Sorry. But you should be wearing nice clothes that look like you put them on on purpose. Does this mean you need to be wearing a blazer? Hell no! But you also shouldn't be wearing sweatpants or a logo T-shirt. What you choose to wear for your author photo might be tied in with your brand.

Think about your brand when taking or choosing an author photo. If your book is horror, a sunny photo from your cruise might not be the right choice. If your book is for children, a suit and tie is probably not the right look because you want to seem approachable and nice. If your book is nonfiction, you don't want to be wearing athleisure. Athleisure doesn't say "I have studied this subject at length." You know how all of Stephen King's author photos feature him in a dark turtleneck glowering through his glasses at the photographer?

Your author photo will also need to be high-resolution (at least 300 dpi/ppi). Do you have a smart phone? Congrats! You have the power to take high-resolution photos. You don't need to hire a photographer or buy a camera; just find a friend who is visually-oriented (maybe they dress sharply or have a nicely decorated house) and hand them your phone.

You know what's not high-resolution? A screenshot of a photo from your Instagram feed. A copy of a copy of a picture. Images are big in terms of digital data, so they get compressed all the time. Even texting a photo you took on your phone to a friend will compress it and make it lower-resolution. Be sure to email or air drop photos and keep them their original size as much as possible.

Using the "zoom" feature on your phone camera can also pixelate an image. It's better to physically move your body to get closer to your subject (or, rather, for your photographer to get closer to you). You can always crop it a bit later if you want.

Your book designer will likely be skilled in Photoshop or a similar program and can clean up small things in your author photo. They're not going to cut three inches from your waist (and they shouldn't; you look amazing, dear). But they can erase blemishes, take the glare off glasses, and brighten the colors. Depending on the photo, they can possibly cut out someone being weird in the background or remove the logo from your shirt. What the designer *can't* do is make a bad image good. They can't make fluorescent overhead lighting look like natural sunlight. They can't make it look like you did your makeup. They aren't magicians.

You could also totally work with a photographer if you'd rather just have a professional handle it. I get it; I *could* change the oil in my car, but I'm not going to. I'm going to hire someone to do that for me. So if you want to do it right and do it well and you feel you can afford to, hire the photographer.

For a great example of a photo of a super attractive author, turn to Page 247.

Author bio

Along with your image, it's common to include a short biography about yourself (along with the illustrator, if applicable). These are typically cursory and sort of boring, but you can jazz yours up a bit if you want to. Work with your project manager and read lots of existing author bios to figure out what works best for you and your book.

Author bios can include—but do not have to include and are not limited to including—the following: education, previous publishing experience, family, hobbies, passions, career, location. There's a lot of room for creativity, here, though, so do what works for you!

For a great example of a wonderfully written biography about a super interesting author, turn to Page 247.

ISBN

ISBN stands for International Standard Book Number. An ISBN is basically your book's social security number, and it helps libraries and retailers keep track of your book numerically. (After all, there are tons of books with the same titles, but they all have unique ISBNs.) ISBNs can be purchased individually or in bulk online. Your publisher will likely obtain yours for you as part of your publishing package; if you're self-publishing, you will have to purchase your own.

If you're considering self-publishing through Amazon, be warned: their ISBNs belong to them alone. Why does that matter?

If you publish your book through Amazon and then later choose to move it elsewhere, you will not be able to bring your ISBN with you. You'll have to buy a new, non-Amazon ISBN and produce a second edition of your book. This is a ton of work that could lead to confusion among your readers. It's better to own your ISBN outright.

Each format and edition of a book has its own ISBN, so your paperback ISBN will be different from your e-book ISBN will be different from your audiobook ISBN. If you ever produce a second edition of your book for any reason, you will need a new ISBN for the new edition.

Your ISBN is a simple purchase that doesn't require any information about your book, so you can buy your ISBN at any time. You should get your number immediately after paying.

LCCN

LCCN stands for Library of Congress Control Number. In America, all books are required to be registered with the Library of Congress. Other countries may have similar programs, so if you're not publishing in the US, do your research to see what you need to do to get your book registered in your country.

You can apply for an LCCN through the Library of Congress's website. This will require you to have a final synopsis, release date, and other information about your book, so it's a good idea to wait until late in your design process to apply for this. Because you apply for an LCCN, it takes a couple days for the Library of Congress to review your application and get you your LCCN. Applying for an LCCN is free.

An LCCN applies to your book in general, so all different formats of your book will have the same LCCN.

After your book is completed and you have some copies, you are required to send one copy to the Library of Congress so they can catalog it along with your LCCN. If you choose to produce an e-book or an alternative print format after applying for your LCCN, you'll need to go back into your account with the Library of Congress and update your copyright accordingly. The only exception to this is audiobooks, as the Library of Congress does not copyright audiobooks at this time.

Cover price

Up until your book is pretty much done being designed, any cover price you've seen has been a best guess. A book's cover price is determined by the page count, format, cover type, size, and other details (which we explored in more detail on Page 107), so it's impossible to know for sure what you're working with until the book is pretty much done. Because of this, you may see your cover price appear on your book cover or be updated from its original estimate late in the design process.

Barcode

Your designer will generate your book's barcode late in the design process. It will be printed on the back cover (sometimes the interior flap of a hard cover's dust jacket) along with your ISBN.

Other formats

All we've reviewed thus far in our production process has been assuming that you are publishing a print book. But the odds are good that you're also producing at least one other format, so let's take a moment to talk about those formats and when they might get produced.

A second print format

If you're publishing both a paperback and a hardcover, your designer will likely have focused on one throughout their design process. They probably laid out your entire paperback book, and each time you've seen it, it's just been the paperback. So where is the hardcover?

Your designer has been working smart *and* hard. They're probably going to use your final paperback files to produce the hardcover files. That is, they're going to make a copy of your paperback files and then adapt those to suit a hardcover. Why would they produce a second design file for a book that's still undergoing changes if they can just wait for everything to be approved?

If you've gotten to the end of your book design process and are expecting a second print format, touch base with your project manager. If your designer hasn't gotten started on that yet, they'll need to soon.

E-book

You're going to want an e-book. That's just the way it is. Your contract should include e-book production, and if it didn't, you're going to want to ask for it. Converting a print book file into an e-book is a relatively simple and easy process, so if everyone has forgotten about it until this moment, it's not too late.

E-books are much like print books in many ways, but there are some differences. Page numbers are removed from pages in e-books, as the Kindle or eReader program automatically generates page numbers as the reader progresses. Because of this, the table of contents is also typically removed or stripped of its page numbers. The barcode comes off the back cover, and any references to the print book may be removed or altered.

There's no good reason not to have an e-book version of your book these days. If you choose not to have an e-book, you will be missing sales.

Audiobook

Not everyone can or wants to "eye-read." Some people with visual impairments or attention disorders may only be able to "ear-read," or listen to audiobooks. Some people with busy schedules may not have time to sit down with a print book and prefer to listen to audiobooks on the go. Some people might just like audiobooks better for no reason whatsoever. Some people might prefer print books but throw in the odd audiobook just to help them get through books faster. All of these are valid reasons to listen to audiobooks, and it's unkind to comment on how another person prefers to read. No reader owes you an explanation of why they read how they do, and none of them are deserving of judgment. Reading is for *everyone* who wants to be a reader.

Some people like to say that listening to audiobooks is not reading. This can be a harmful thing to say to or about someone with a disability that makes it hard for them to eye-read. Imagine you cannot physically read with your eyes, so you listen to audiobooks instead, and some ass on the internet is really adamant that it's "not really reading." What is reading? Experiencing a new story; immersing yourself in a new world. Listening to audiobooks is a type of reading, and it's extremely unkind to comment on how another person prefers to read. (Déjà vu? I said this two times because it's important.)

What does this have to do with you? Your book should have an audiobook! If you can afford it and your project manager supports it, you should work together to produce an audiobook. This will open your book up to a whole host of new ear-readers who might not be able to engage with your book otherwise.

You may narrate your own audiobook, or you may hire someone to narrate it for you. That narrator or their company may also edit those audio files so they sound clean and crisp; you may have to hire a separate editor. Your publisher may have an in-house editor.

Work with your project manager to come up with an audiobook attack plan. You owe it to yourself and your readers.

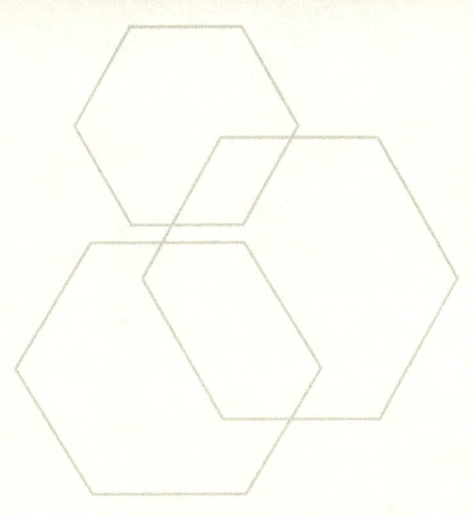

3
Reviewing and Finalizing

<u>Final review</u>

Once your book is "done," it will be reviewed by several parties to ensure you're sending the best book possible to the printer. You may believe your book is totally complete, so it might feel like a strange pause right at the end of production when your book goes through its rounds of reviews. However, the fact of the matter is that the final reviews are the most important phase of your book's production, so this step is not to be rushed.

Project manager review

Your project manager will review your book one final time to make sure details like your LCCN, ISBN, and cover price are all correct. They will also review formatting and double-check for consistency. They may not reread your entire book, but they'll certainly check their own work before passing it along to another editor.

Editorial review

An editor—often a third editor, not your primary editor (who was possibly your project manager) and not your proofreader—will review your book to double-check details like your LCCN, ISBN, and cover price. They'll also review for consistency in formatting.

Author review

The author will review the book's design files one last time and request any final corrections. Corrections at this phase should be exclusively mechanical or spelling, or in the name of clarity. This is certainly not the time to be replacing "say" with "utter" just because you like it better. This is the time to catch any last glaring errors. You will confirm your final approval by signing a print release[22].

---

22   *print release: a document an author signs acknowledging that they believe their book is ready to go to print*

Metadata

Metadata is all of the information about your book that will help distributors, stores, and even readers to understand and categorize your book. Your project manager will pull together a list of all of your metadata, and you'll probably never need to look at it. But for those who are self-publishing, or for those who simply like to know what's going on, here's a brief overview of what your book's metadata may include:

Item	Description
Book title	Duh.
Subtitle (if applicable)	A subtitle comes after the title, typically after a colon (:), and is often seen in nonfiction books. The subtitle should elaborate upon the title.
Author(s)	The author and possibly a co-author or collection of authors
Non-author contributors (if applicable)	This may include a ghostwriter, illustrator, translator, or another person not on the publishing team who substantively affected your book.
Publisher/ Imprint	This may be the name of your publishing company (Wildling Press) or an imprint of a larger publishing company (like Tor, an imprint of Macmillan).
ISBN	International Standard Book Number. This is basically your book's global social security number. You'll definitely be assigned an ISBN-13 (thirteen digits), and you may also be assigned an ISBN-10 (ten digits).

Item	Description
LCCN	Library of Congress Control Number. American books are required to be registered with the Library of Congress. Other countries may have other similar registrations.
Trim size	This is the size your book is designed to fit. Some common sizes are 8.5x8.5" (often for children's picture), 5x8" (often for novels), and 6x9" (often for nonfiction).
Cover finish	Either glossy (shiny) or matte (not shiny)
Format(s)	What formats is your book going to be published in? Hardcover (casebound or dust jacket?), paperback, e-book, audiobook?
Genre	Think basic. This will be more like "fantasy" than "vibey epic high diverse fantasy."
Age range/ grade range	This is for juvenile books; adult books are just labeled "adult."
Launch date	The official release date for your book
Elevator book description	Your final one-sentence book description
Full book description	Your final full-length book synopsis, often what appears on your back cover (or dust flap)
Endorsements	A list of any and all endorsements you've received (character limit notwithstanding)
Author bio	A brief, third-person, official bio of the author
Author photo	This will certainly have been approved by your project manager long before it was inserted in your book!

"Juvenile" books include board books for babies, children's picture books, early chapter books, more substantial middle grade books, and even thick young adult novels! If the target audience is under eighteen (adult lovers of YA aside), the book is "juvenile."

Item	Description
BISAC subject codes	These are Book Industry Standards and Communications categories as determined by the Book Industry Study Group (BISG). You or your project manager will visit the subjects website (https://bisg.org/page/BISACEdition) and browse around to find the three most appropriate categories for your book. Each category will have an accompanying code. For example, the three BISAC subject codes for this book are: • BUS070060 BUSINESS & ECONOMICS / Industries / Media & Communications • LAN027000 LANGUAGE ARTS & DISCIPLINES / Publishers & Publishing Industry • LAN005020 LANGUAGE ARTS & DISCIPLINES / Writing / Business Aspects
Thema subject codes	A Thema subject is basically just your book's theme. In many ways, these codes are similar to BISAC subject codes, except that they're published by EDItEUR. You'll have to simply root around on the website (https://ns.editeur.org/thema/en_) to find the Thema subject codes that work best for your book. For example, the three Thema subject codes for this book are: • KNTP1 Publishing and book trade • KJS Sales and marketing • CBW Writing and editing guides

As you can see, the BISAC subjects are broader, and each of them applies to the whole of this book. However, the Thema subjects are more specific and therefore three are required to fully describe the breadth of what this book covers.

Proofs

This is another exciting phase of production that requires lots of patience. The designer will upload your book files to the printer, who will then screen them for technical issues. If there are any issues, the printer will reject the files, and the designer will remedy the errors. At this stage, the only issues that might arise would be technical details of your book's design file. If there are no issues, the printer will accept the files and send the designer a soft proof.

Soft proof

Once the printer has approved the book files, they will send your publisher a soft proof, also known as a digital proof. This is a PDF file that simply confirms that everything was received correctly by the printer. Since this proof is digital, the printer often turns it around within a few days. It won't come in minutes, and it also shouldn't take two weeks. Your designer and project manager will both review your soft proof, and if everything looks good, the designer will order a printer's proof.

Printer's proof

A printer's proof is a single print copy of your book in each of its formats. The purpose of the printer's proof is to ensure that every element of your book looks the same in real life as it did on the computer. You will want to inspect placement, check colors, flip through the interior, and generally just make sure that everything is as it should be.

Your publisher will probably order one or two printer's proofs. Your project manager will review one copy, checking that everything looks the same in print as it did on their screen. They or another editor will read your book from cover to cover to check for any persistent glaring errors. Your publisher will send the second printer's proof along to you! (Some publishers may only order one printer's proof and send it to you after they've reviewed it from cover to cover.)

It's normal for authors to grow impatient at this stage, as it can feel like you're so close to the finish line but screeching to a dead stop. However, it's extremely important not to rush any of these final steps. The final review is crucial to making sure the book you release into the world is excellent and accurate. Seeing a book in print is a different experience than looking at it on a computer. You and your editor have been looking at the same pages for so long, your brains have grown fatigued of it. So reviewing the physical proof is not a step that can be rushed or skipped.

If your project manager has noted any changes that need to be made, they will bring those to your attention. If you catch any glaring errors, your project manager will likely be happy to fix those. They may opt not to enact changes that are not glaring errors, as the time for text changes will have been long past by now. Defer to your project manager's judgment on whether changes are worth making at this stage.

If these changes are substantial, your publisher may choose to order a revised printer's proof. Ordering a revised printer's proof may set back your book's release date, but the risk of skipping this step is sometimes too high to take. Surely, while you want your book to be done, you more so want it to be done *correctly.*

Colors

Let's talk about color expectations. Screens are typically set to an RGB color mode, and printers print using CMYK. What do all these letters mean? Well, RGB is additive; the more color you add, the whiter the color gets. Because of this, RGB can produce brighter colors. Printers use CMYK colors, which is subtractive; the more color you add, the closer the color gets to black. CMYK can produce a muddier tone, especially in very dark color illustrations. When you see neon in print, a spot color has been chosen, and special, pre-mixed ink (read: more expensive) has been used. Digital printers (Page 128) do not typically use ink conducive to creating brilliant neon or metallic colors.

It's also important to remember that screens are backlit by their own light, so they will always show colors brighter than how they will print. This needs to be kept in mind when setting expectations for the final printed book. If you're publishing a novel or another "adult" book, you won't have to worry much. But it's a good idea to temper your expectations and plan your illustrations according to this difference in printing.

Approval

Once the printer's proof has been approved by the author and the publisher, your publisher will approve your book with their printer. Once the printer knows the book is approved, it will enable your book for global distribution so it can be purchased through book retailers. More on that on Page 135.

Offset printing

We have not yet talked about digital versus offset printing, and that's because digital printing is almost always the way to go. Digitally printing a book is very like printing a document off your home printer, except much better quality. A digital printer takes your book's file and simply prints it, whether you want one copy or a hundred.

An offset printer is more like the printing presses of yore, where the printing press is physically set to your book's design. Because this involves a ton of work in setting up the press, offset printing requires that several hundred copies are ordered all at once. (Typically, at least a thousand copies are required to make offset printing financially worthwhile.)

Due to the huge upfront investment needed to print a thousand or more copies offset, digital printing is almost always preferred. However, some books may be produced offset. If your book is being produced offset, you'll definitely want to speak to your project manager about how that process will differ from digital printing as it's been outlined here.

FUN FACT

Digital printing is also called "print on demand." Some people in the publishing industry look down on printing on demand because it's wrapped up with the stigma against indie and self-publishing. For most authors these days, it's the only viable option and perfectly sufficient for their needs.

Offset Printing Pros and Cons

Pros	Cons
• The paper quality is better and therefore the image quality is sharper. • Price per book can decrease when purchasing bulk quantities.	• Offset printers do not typically distribute or work with distributors to distribute your book, so you'll need to handle distribution on your own or through a separate distributor. • Printing can take much longer, as the process is more involved and the quantity is higher. • Very large quantities must be ordered upfront, which can lead to unsold copies sitting around your garage.

Who should print offset?

Offset printing is not for the faint of heart. It's a long, complicated process in addition to all of the rest of your book's production you just went through. But in some specific cases, the final product will only look good if it's printed offset.

Books that contain lots of photos or art should be printed offset. An oversized coffee table book featuring a series of photographs or a school yearbook needs to be printed offset to achieve the crispness and vividness of the images it centers on. Children's or other illustrated books set in dark tones would do better printed offset.

It's important to note that some publishers may not offer offset printing at all, since it's so much more involved than digital printing. If you feel certain you want your book to be printed offset, seek out a publisher who offers that or seems to offer it. If they've published other books with lots of high-resolution images, they can likely publish yours.

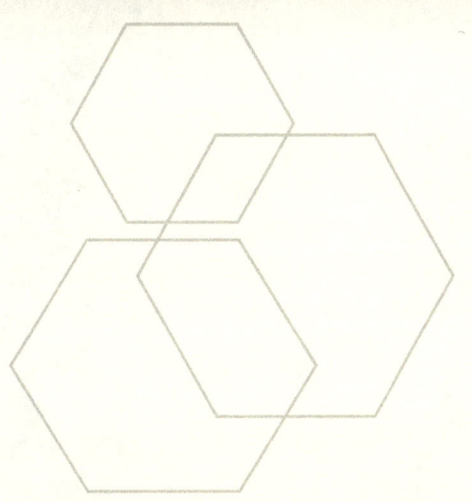

4
Distribution

You've written the book, you've chosen your publishing path, you've worked with an editor, you've had someone design it, and you've signed off that it's done and done! So that's it, right?

Sure—for the most part. But there are a lot of behind-the-curtain steps that need to take place after your book is "finished" to get it into stores. Once your book is complete, it won't just magically appear on Amazon. It will need to be distributed there by a distributor.

What's a distributor? When it comes to books and a lot of other products, a distributor is a company responsible for taking your completed product from your printer and getting it out into the world. They act sort of like a glorified shipping company, schlepping your books from A to B so you don't have to worry about it.

Working with a distributor can be quite complex, and every company is different. The good news is that many distributors these days work with their own printers in tandem to both print your books and get them where they need to be as part of the same system. Ingram Book Group, one of the largest and most

FUN FACT

Remember we mentioned IngramSpark on Page 32 as a great self-publishing service? It's also owned by Ingram Book Group!

prevalent book distributors in the world, also owns and operates LightningSource, who prints all its books. You don't have to work with Ingram and then move to working with LightningSource; they're the same company and you use them the same way. This duality is by far the most straightforward way to make your books and get them out into the world.

You'd need to look for your own distributor if you're printing your books offset, which we briefly went over on Page 128. If you're printing your books offset, you'll be well aware of having made that choice, and hopefully your publisher or printer would be able to guide you in choosing and engaging with a distributor, or even do it on your behalf. You may also need a separate international distributor if you wish to sell in a country that your printer does not automatically distribute to.

Where are books distributed?

When you work with a printer/distributor combo like Ingram/LightningSource, they take care of everything. Your publisher—or possibly you, if you're self-publishing, or whomever is helping you—has already uploaded your book to the printer, along with its metadata. So then your printer/distributor will turn around and send your book out into the world.

When your book is approved with your printer, your distributor will start blasting it out to online retailers. Sometimes this "blast" doesn't happen all at once, so in the beginning, you might see some strange errors like missing cover images, "Out of stock" instead of "Available for pre-order," or your hardcover and paperback showing up as if they're two unrelated books. Almost always, these issues resolve themselves within a few days as the online retailers get more information.

Retailers

Amazon

We're not here to criticize Amazon as a concept (but maybe check out the section about Bookshop on Page 141). Love it or hate it, your book needs to be available for sale through Amazon, as it accounts for at least half (HALF!) of all (ALL!) book sales. The odds are good that an overwhelming majority of your book sales will come from Amazon. That's just what Amazon does: it sells things. In fact, the company sold exclusively books when it was originally founded in 1994 as Relentless.com.

We're not here to pass judgment about Amazon . . . but you have to admit it's a better name than Relentless.

Your book will certainly be made available on Amazon if you use any reputable distributor. Through Amazon, just about anyone in the world can have your book in its printed format sitting on their stoop within two days from the push of a button (assuming your book has officially released).

Beyond that, Amazon has revolutionized the accessibility of books to all kinds of people with financial, visual, or other disadvantages. Through Amazon, booklovers with small budgets can find excellent deals and buy books at half the cover price or less at no loss to the authors. Through Amazon, Kindle Unlimited subscribers can rent your book at zero additional cost to them. Through Amazon, people with different seeing abilities can access your audiobook through Audible and have your work delivered directly into their ears. Through Amazon, books with no audiobook can still be downloaded in e-book format and read aloud by the AI support on Kindle.

Amazon is providing access to booklovers and stifling book sales from other retailers at the same time. Both things are true. We are not here to take a stance on Amazon. Odds are good you bought this book on Amazon. That is just fine (but explore Bookshop with us on Page 141). However, it is a simple fact that Amazon is the number-one powerhouse of capitalism, and if you want to sell books, you need to harness its platform.

Amazon book pages

You probably know that any Amazon product page can contain a lot of information. A book page is no different or possibly even more hectic than a typical Amazon product page. It's so important that a potential buyer is able to clearly and easily find your book's synopsis and other important details like its genre and age group. All of these details are available through Amazon's book pages.

By this point, you've already uploaded all your metadata to your distributor, and they have in turn sent it to Amazon. When your book listing appears on Amazon, closely review the book page to ensure all information is correct (after waiting for it to populate fully, of course). If any of your book's information is wrong or could be presented more clearly, connect with your publicist or project manager to review your book's metadata.

Amazon reviews

They're the best of things; they're the worst of things. Amazon reviews can really make or break a book, and it's up to the author and the publicist to make sure the reviews they solicit are makers and not breakers.

Anyone can review any item on Amazon. Nearly all non-book reviews are to comment on the quality of the item. "Thick fabric," "solid base," "not the same color as pictured," etc. Books are one of the rare categories on Amazon where people leave reviews based on personal opinion about the content rather than physical qualities about the item. This is due to the five-star rating system that book review apps like Goodreads and book retailers like Amazon share. A book can be perfectly produced and printed, but a consumer may still not enjoy it due to personal taste and rate it two stars.

Equally frustrating is the absolutely subjective nature of these ratings. There are hundreds of Amazon book reviews out there that say, "Loved it, great book," and then give only four stars. Or, worse, someone might say something like, "I thought this was a kids' book!" in a review about a book that was clearly labeled as adult fiction, and that person might leave a book a one-star rating, and there is nothing the author can do about that.

This sucks! Why even try to do anything about book reviews, if people can just say whatever they want to? Well, Amazon, for better or for worse, really matters, and consumers who use Amazon read the reviews, or at least glance at the average star rating. What can we do about Amazon reviews to help your book look good despite those rogue reviewers? The only answer is to get as many positive reviews as possible to drown out the bad ones.

Authors must solicit Amazon reviews however they can. There are a ton of ways to ask readers to leave an Amazon review. You can add a page to the back of your book asking readers who enjoyed the book to leave a review. When someone comments that they enjoyed your book, you can ask them to leave those exact thoughts as an Amazon review. You can send email blasts asking for reviews or distribute bookmarks along with book orders you're personally processing asking for Amazon reviews. There are a ton of ways to solicit Amazon reviews, and authors should be doing several of them.

Anyone can leave a review for any item on Amazon, even if they haven't bought it through Amazon. Those who have purchased that item through Amazon are labeled as a "verified purchase," which means little when it comes to books. So even if you gave a copy of your book to someone for free, they can still leave you an Amazon review.

Take every opportunity to seek Amazon reviews. A book with five thousand reviews sells better than a book with five; a book with a five-star rating sells better than a book with a three-star rating. Set a goal for yourself for how many Amazon reviews you want to earn in your first week or month after your book's release date.

Amazon's bookish subsidiaries

Amazon doesn't own *everything* . . . but it's close. Amazon owns a ton of subsidiaries, including some that you probably thought were independent—or at least free from Amazon ownership. But there are a couple of bookish subsidiaries of Amazon that make books more accessible to more readers that you're probably already at least slightly familiar with.

Kindle

Amazon Kindle is Amazon's e-book platform. A Kindle is a physical device, a tablet people use to read e-books. Kindle is the online platform where those books can be shopped for, purchased, and ultimately accessed for reading.

Kindles are specifically designed for reading e-books. They can do other tasks, like access the internet, play games, and use apps, but they are designed first and foremost for readers to read on. Kindles have been around since 2007, so there are a lot of different versions, and they just keep getting more and more advanced. The most recent iterations of the Kindle have special features like anti-glare screens, annotating and note-taking tools, and lightweight frames.

Kindle is also a section of Amazon's online platform where you can browse and buy e-books. Some readers have vast digital libraries all contained in one small device. They can save their notes, track their progress, and view their library with ease all in one place. Some readers love the convenience and cost-effectiveness of Kindles, while others prefer to hoard print books. Both are extremely valid options, and it's not kind to comment on how another person prefers to read.

Audible

Many audiobooks are distributed through Amazon's audiobook arm, Audible. Audible is a membership-only program, meaning that readers can't just pop in and purchase an audiobook. They must be signed up to a monthly Audible subscription. The "plus" subscription gives subscribers a small pool of audiobooks they can listen to all they want; the "premium" subscription additionally grants members one audiobook download per month, which must be chosen from a long but not comprehensive list of their available audiobooks. Any additional audiobooks, or those not included on that list, must be purchased in addition to the monthly membership fees.

If you produce an audiobook for your book, you'll want it to be available through Audible. About forty percent of audiobooks are distributed through Audible. Amazon even has its own audiobook production studio called ACX that makes uploading audiobooks to Amazon very easy and straightforward.

Goodreads

Goodreads is owned by Amazon, so we wanted to be sure to mention it here. However, Goodreads does not facilitate direct sales, so learn more about it in our section about non-retail places where books are discussed on Page 149.

Bookshop

Bookshop is the independent bookselling industry's response to Amazon. For a long time, the only way to purchase books from an independent retailer was to physically walk into your local bookstore and hope they had the title you were looking for. Bookstores are magical places full of great books and often even better people, but due to the fact that shelf space is limited and there are millions of books in the world, they can't always carry the exact book a buyer is looking for. They could perhaps place a special order for that specific book, but that would involve the buyer waiting for the order to come in and possibly even driving back to the store a second time to pick that book up.

Bookshop.org is really the first retailer to fill this industry need for independently sold books that are easy to purchase. And since this company launched in January of 2020, we can thank the COVID-19 pandemic for driving its popularity as book readers were hesitant to walk into physical stores to look for books.

Bookshop is a retailer that sells books they receive from the distributor, just like Amazon. Just like Amazon, they have fast shipping times (not two-day, but fast; that two-day shipping window is nearly impossible to achieve and sustain, and it has led to many contemporary criticisms of Amazon, like employee abuse and a high carbon footprint). However, there are a couple crucial differences between Bookshop and Amazon.

Amazon is The Monopoly. If you looked up "monopoly" in the dictionary, Amazon's logo would be directly underneath. Amazon's founder, Jeffrey Bezos, is worth an estimated $162.3 billion at the time of writing. Amazon's only goal is to make and keep money. They have so much money they don't even always make you return the item you're returning; they just give you the money back.

We're not here to bash Amazon, but we are here to uplift Bookshop. Bookshop's main amazing feature is that it shares its profits with independent bookstores. Thirty percent of a purchase's retail value (not Bookshop's profit; the entire retail value) goes to independent bookstores. Bookshop consumers can even designate which independent bookstore they would like their purchases to support, so they can support their neighborhood bookstore or a friend's bookstore or a bookstore in need.

Bookshop also facilitates customer service on these book purchases. Amazon's customer service is laughable, as they are so vast and profitable they simply don't need to care about imbuing any kind of personal touch in their customer interactions. No matter what Amazon does, people will use it, and that much has been demonstrated at length over the years since its founding in 1994.

Bookshop, on the other hand, provides quick and compassionate support to its customers and its publishers and authors!

Bookshop makes a special point to highlight books in subjects that matter to contemporary readers; Amazon merely highlights whatever is selling well. On Bookshop's homepage, you'll find lists of recommendations by subject. At the time of writing, its homepage features "Books for Leaving Social Media," "Start Local," "Latinx Releases," and "Books for Budding Authors" to help kids learn to love writing. Bookshop goes out of its way to rotate its recommendations and incorporate everyone into those lists, including those authors whose voices have historically been marginalized.

This final point is, of course, completely subjective, but Bookshop is also endlessly more user-friendly than Amazon. Amazon's item pages are cluttered and confusing with so much information a consumer has a hard time finding the information they actually need. A book page on Bookshop is simple: price and formats, synopsis, book details, and author bio, all in a row. The crisp, clean white design is a joy to browse.

This section was not meant to be a persuasive essay, and yet here we are. Bookshop is an incredible independent retailer who shares its profits with smaller independent retailers. They are far more concerned with community than with capitalism. They uplift marginalized voices, highlight books that contemporary readers are looking for, and celebrate their freedom from the yoke of Amazon. If you can wait ten days instead of two for your book, if you can afford only a couple dollars off the cover price rather than the cover price cut in half, opt to shop Bookshop.

Barnes and Noble

Barnes and Noble is this middle ground between independent bookstores and Amazon. Back in the nineties, Barnes and Noble (along with the late Borders) held the market monopoly on book sales. There was a time when Barnes and Noble and Borders (RIP) were pretty much the only places a person would think to buy a book.

Nowadays, "monopoly" means something totally different. Barnes and Noble, in terms of gross profit, is nothing compared to Amazon, Walmart, Target, or Costco. So the contemporary book buyer views Barnes and Noble with nostalgia and compassion. They want to protect Barnes and Noble from meeting the same fate as Borders. This, combined with the substantial uptick in reading in general since the beginning of the COVID-19 pandemic, has stabilized Barnes and Noble's place among the bookselling titans of the twenty-first century.

Barnes and Noble has come to be considered a bit of a classic bookseller. They have an important place in bookish culture. You can walk into a physical store in every state except Wyoming (come on, Wyoming!), and you can easily purchase books on their website. They stock just about every book and host book signings. Their locations can support indie authors, but they don't go out of their way to do so. Basically, they're bookselling vanilla, and that is just fine and we love them for it.

When you distribute your book through a global distribution

network like Ingram, it will automatically be distributed to Barnes and Noble. This means that your book will be available for purchase through their website; this also means that their physical stores are literally capable of stocking your book. This does *not* mean you will suddenly find your book on the shelves of every Barnes and Noble location like magic.

Shelf space is extremely limited in bookstores. The average Barnes and Noble will be larger than a typical independent bookstore, but it can still only hold a couple thousand books. There have been maybe? three? million? books published ever. We must ask ourselves—and I mean this with all due respect—why on Earth should they stock *your* book? Yours, of all people? Out of THREE? MILLION? BOOKS? Former President Obama wrote a book. Dolly Parton wrote a book. Why should a bookstore stock your book?

That's the ultimate question of life, the universe, and everything for an author.

The best way to get Barnes and Noble—or any bookstore—to stock physical copies of your book and put them on their shelves is for you to host an event there. When you host a book signing or reading at a Barnes and Noble, that's an indication to them that you may bring in people who want to buy that book. It's high risk to stock books written by some local author you've never heard of. What if they never sell? It's only a medium risk to stock books written by some local author who is willing to come be part of your brand for an hour or two and encourage people to come to your store. It's very low risk to stock books written by Obama. Those puppies will *sell*.

You can also totally approach your local Barnes and Noble locations to see if they have any methods of supporting local authors. Maybe they have a local author section or can put a "local author" tag on your book. Some may be eager to help you; some may say, "I'll pass your information along to my supervisor," and then not. It's up to you and your publicist to see each of these encounters through and figure out next steps.

So, expect to see your book available for pre-order and eventually for purchase at www.barnesandnoble.com. Expect it to look good there, reputable, "like a real book" on the website of this most classic of book retailers. But if you, a debut independent author, want to see your book on Barnes and Noble's shelves, you're going to have to work for that. You and your publicist are going to need to ask each store individually.

Big box stores

If you use a global book distributor like Ingram, your book will also automatically show up on the websites of some of the biggest Western retailers, like Walmart, Costco, Target, etc. The book sections of these stores are small compared to the stores themselves; to call their shelf space "limited" would be a laughable understatement. These companies are so large and so general that they don't care much about one specific department. So they tend to stock the bestsellers, and they sell those bestsellers to their very general audience.

This isn't to say you shouldn't ask if they'll stock your book. Always ask. Asking is the only way you can get anything done in this world. But don't be surprised when they say no. At least your book is on their website!

Independent booksellers

It's hard to write about independent booksellers because there are so many wonderful ones out there who are all so different. But we can probably agree that independent booksellers are amazing, magical, crucial, brilliant, comforting institutions—not to be dramatic. The cozy, quaint, fierce independent bookstore is one of the most romanticized images in the modern world.

It's hard to be an independent bookstore, just like it's hard to be an independent author. Both must advocate for themselves; both must fight against the big boys at the tops of their industries; both must work nonstop to realize and continue realizing their dreams. Because of this, it's crucially important that independent authors and bookstores commit to mutually supporting one another.

Partner with your local bookstores however you can, not because you want to sell your book, but because you want to be part of their community. Ask if they'll sell books at your book launch party (which would benefit them as they'd get to keep the profits; it would benefit you as you'd get to enjoy your day and not worry about sales). Offer to host events in the store (and then give those events your all). Gas them up on social media (and share their content!). Use their links in your email newsletters (especially if they so kindly agreed to stock your book!). Select them as your preferred bookstore on Bookshop (and Libro.fm). Celebrate your local bookstores however and whenever you can, and be grateful you have them! In exchange, hopefully they will be grateful to stock your wonderful book.

In terms of distribution, indie bookstores work a bit differently from the big retailers like Amazon and Walmart. Amazon and Walmart have massive, automated processes that bring your book from Ingram (or your other distributor) into their system and onto their website. Indie bookstores don't have this system, however, and most of them probably wouldn't want it.

An indie bookstore will typically have their own bookseller account with Ingram, and they'll have to go in and manually order your book. You see the trouble with this? They have to both know your book exists and believe that they can make money from stocking and selling it to take this step and order your book on purpose. It's up to you to make all of this happen.

When it's about time to start publicizing your book, go around and introduce yourself to all your local bookstores; take a copy of your book with you. Say hello to whomever is at the desk and make them your new friend. Tell them a bit about yourself and about your book. Ask how they like to connect with local authors. With any luck, you'll get to speak to the owner, manager, or events planner about how you can mutually support one another.

Non-retailer sites

Your book will also show up on some bookish websites that aren't designed for outright purchasing, but rather for booklovers to connect and share and log information.

Goodreads

Goodreads is a book social media app where users can keep track of what books they've read, post their reviews and ratings, and access new book recommendations. While authors can't sell their books directly through Goodreads, there are lots of ways to drive book sales using this app.

Goodreads hosts many ongoing book giveaways. When app users enter a book giveaway, the Goodreads default is to mark that book as "to be read" on their accounts. Even if a person doesn't win your book, they may remember it later and even see it on their "to be read" list.

Goodreads allows authors to publish lots of additional material to accompany their book. They can host question and answer events, talk about their writing process, or post old drafts of a now published and beloved book.

Goodreads is also crucially important to authors in the rating and review department. Many book readers forgo reading the Amazon item reviews of a book they're considering buying in favor of reading the Goodreads reviews, the logic being that Goodreads is populated by avid readers rather than laypersons and therefore they may have opinions that more closely align with another avid reader. In the same way that authors must pursue Amazon reviews, they should also pursue Goodreads reviews.

Storygraph

As you have perhaps picked up on, we love supporting indie creators and businesses. While Goodreads is not a commerce site, it is owned by Amazon, and it's certainly a more independent move to not be owned by Amazon. For those who prefer not to use Goodreads, there's Storygraph.

Storygraph is new, launched in June 2021. The app's design is extremely user-friendly, sleek, and neat, with lots of fun features. Because they're brand new, they're quick to fix bugs and eager to involve their community in their development moving forward. A Storygraph user can set an annual reading goal, track what they've read, leave reviews and ratings, and chat with other readers. They can also view their personal reading data—what mood, genre, page count, and format they prefer, and beyond—and view book recommendations based on their past data or a specific mood they're seeking. Those who wish to convert from Goodreads to Storygraph can import their data so they don't lose track of what they've read.

Storygraph is just one more excellent app readers can use to avoid the Amazon machine. Its founders are also its main employees, both people of color and booklovers themselves. The app is very pretty to look at and easy to use. We're not here to bash Goodreads . . . we're just here to tell everyone how awesome Storygraph is.

IndieBound

IndieBound was the predecessor of Bookshop for those readers who were desperate to harness the immense power of the internet to purchase indie books. Created by the American Booksellers Association in 2008, IndieBound allows users to search for a specific book and determine which of their local bookstores sells it. This site also offers to redirect buyers to Bookshop.

Wholesale discounts

A wholesale discount is the percentage discount off the cover price someone can purchase your book for directly from the distributor. By "someone," we're not talking about individual book buyers; we're talking about you, your publisher, bookstores, and other "bulk" orders. "Bulk" is in quotation marks here because you don't actually have to purchase a bulk quantity of your book to receive the wholesale discount. It's yet another benefit of publishing your book digitally that you get the wholesale discount on any purchase from one to one thousand books. However, it's helpful to conceptualize who might buy your book "in bulk" as opposed to a single person buying a single copy.

When you are or your publisher is uploading your book to the printer, they get to select what the wholesale discount should be. Typically, a wholesale discount will be 50% to 55% off the cover price. Retailers can see through their Ingram accounts what your wholesale discount is set at, and they take this into consideration along with other details about your book. Some retailers won't stock any book with a discount of lower than 55% off the cover price. This is important to keep in mind when setting your wholesale discount. As always, if you're confused or need advice, consult your project manager.

What is pre-order?

Between when your book is finished and when it releases, it will be available for "pre-order." This time period might also be referred to as your "soft launch" or your "limited release." This is when your book exists, but like, not really. You and your publisher might have copies of the book; retailers might be stocking them up, getting ready for the big day; reviewers might have started receiving copies so they can read the book and craft their reviews ahead of time. But regular people can't just get your book; they have to wait for the release date.

Readers can pre-order books through pretty much any of the retailers we've spoken about so far. They "add to cart" and "check out" like a regular book purchase, knowing that book will not ship to their home for several months. Typically, retailers mail out books a couple days before the official release date, hoping that'll land those books on stoops on day of. This is certainly an imperfect art, but they do what they can.

This period is also when you must start promoting your book in absolutely every way conceivable. The more people who pre-order your book, the higher you'll rank in lists, the more you'll show up in people's recommendations, the more reviewers you'll have right away, the more people will buy your book. Drive as many people as you can to the pre-order.

How? you might ask. By publicizing your book, of course!

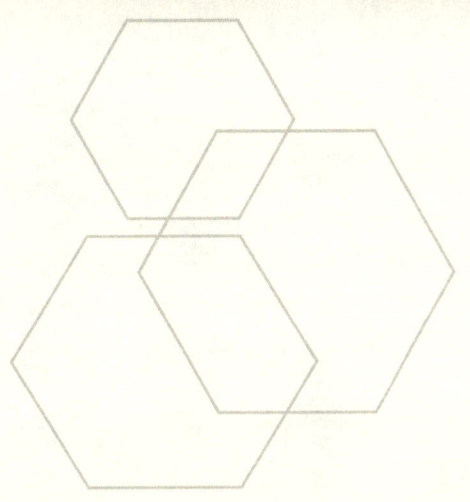

5
Marketing

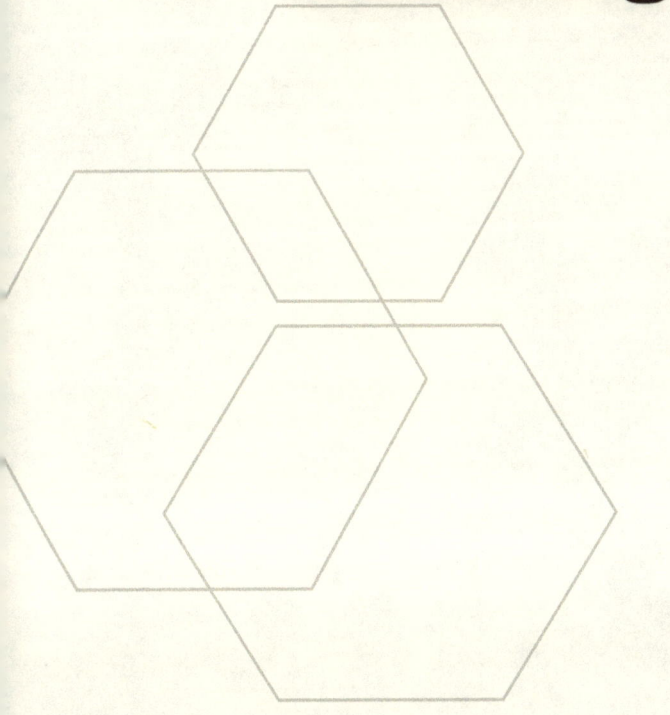

Advertising, publicity, public relations, promotion, and marketing

For the most part, people tend to use all or some of these terms interchangeably, and that's totally fine. However, there are differences here that may be important as you start trying to spread the news about your book into the world.

Advertising is perhaps the easiest to identify. If you're looking at an ad, that's advertising. Advertising usually focuses solely on trying to sell an item, and this is usually done through online ads, billboards, signs, magazine and other print ads, and direct mailing. Advertising is by far the salesiest item on this list.

Publicity is media coverage. When your book is available for pre-order and your publicist sends out a press release to news outlets, that's publicity. Publicity includes reviews and features published about you and your book in print or digital publications.

Public relations has to do with your image or your overall brand, which we talk about more on Page 196. The way the public perceives you and how that brand ties into your ultimate goal of selling books or spreading your message are all part of public relations.

Promotion is getting your book in front of people's eyeballs. Promotion can look like social media posts, website updates, email newsletters, and more that connect you to your audience. Through these avenues, your ongoing conversation about your book and its status and achievements constitute promotion.

Marketing is all of these things; it's the bubble under which these more nuanced activities live. Because of this, to talk about "book marketing" is perfectly reasonable, as you'll likely use more than one of these approaches when it's time to spread the word about your upcoming book.

In theory, much of what you and your publicist will be doing will be promotion. The goal will be to keep your book relevant by keeping the conversation around it energized. However, public relations is an important arm of your work here, as the way you conduct yourself online and interact with your audience all circle back into public relations. You'll also likely engage in some level of publicity and advertising on your journey.

Early marketing

Early marketing is the work you can do for yourself as an author and your book before the book is scheduled for release. There is a ton of marketing work you can set up ahead of time so when your book launches, you get to focus on the celebration without stressing about whether all your ducks are in a row. Early marketing ensures that when you finally have a cover reveal, schedule your release date, or post your book's preorder link, you already have an audience to share the news with!

When is the right time to start marketing your book?

It's a trick question. The right time to start marketing yourself as an author and your book is while you're drafting, before you have a publishing contract, before your book can really even be called a book. If you missed that window, don't worry; your time to get started is now.

Website

An author's website is their "home" on the internet, where readers and potential readers can find the book(s), learn more about the author, and stay up to date on their latest news. It's important for an author to have a website; beyond its practicality, it also demonstrates that you have technical literacy and understanding.

That isn't to say you should plan to design your website yourself. It's a good idea to hire someone to make your website for you, consistent with your branding. However, for those authors who are technologically savvy, you can totally make your own website pretty easily through Weebly, Wix, Squarespace, and other drag-and-drop website design platforms.

Either way, you'll need to choose a domain name, aka your URL, aka your web address. This should be short, simple, and straightforward. Something like www.yourname.com is great; if your name is unavailable, try www.yournameauthor.com or else www.yourname-books.com. Don't get jazzy here unless you have to.

A typical author website will include a homepage that overviews the rest of the contents, a book page with ordering information (including links to online retailers like Bookshop, Barnes and Noble, and Amazon), a blog and updates page, and an author page featuring the author's bio and contact information. Lots of other pages can be added if necessary, but generally an author website needs to start with these items.

You can either make a good website and let it lie, or you can consistently update it with new information. All you really need is to be findable online. When people can find your website easily, they can find your book easily.

Email marketing

Many marketing experts say that the best way to connect with your audience is to grow and nurture a stellar email list. Through email marketing, you can reach readers directly in their own inboxes. You can also stay connected to your existing readers who may be likely to purchase your next book or attend your events.

Choosing a platform

There are lots of ways to go about email marketing, but all of them start with an email marketing platform. You may have heard of MailChimp, Constant Contact, Mailer Lite, or others. Some are simple; some are complex. Some are old; some are new. Some are paid; some are free; some are free up until a point and then they start charging. They all serve the basic purpose of helping you collect email addresses and distribute emails. Do some research, maybe sign up for some free trials, to figure out which platform is best for you.

Building your list

Start your email list with friends and family. With their permission, add their emails to your account. You can also collect emails through your website, whether on a certain page or perhaps a pop-up that appears on the homepage. You can collect emails in person at events or over the internet in other ways when you do virtual events.

You may choose to organize your email subscribers into lists, like those who are local and those who aren't, or those who are interested in your historical fiction novels and those who are interested in your picture books. It's only valuable to separate subscribers in this way if you plan to send different content to each list. Otherwise, it's easier to just lump them all together.

The only thing that truly matters when you're building your email list is consent. Never add someone to your email list without their permission (except maybe like your mom). I am so serious about this. Think about how annoying it is to get emails you didn't sign up for. Don't be an annoying inbox monster. Always, always get consent before adding anyone to your email list.

Sending your emails

The best way to figure out how you want your email marketing to work is to sign up for other authors' emails. You may choose to only send emails when something noteworthy has come up, or you may want to email every Friday. You might share bookish updates only, or perhaps you want to treat it more like a blog and write something longer. Really, it's up to you, and the best approach to email marketing is the one you'll actually do.

Final thoughts about email marketing

This has been an extremely cursory approach to email marketing, and there is so much more to be said about it. The cool thing is, I don't have to say it, because someone else already has. I recommend *Newsletter Ninja: How to Become an Author Mailing List Expert* by Tammi Labrecque. Because there are so many different platforms, each with their own functions and features, it's hard to write briefly and generally about this subject. However, email marketing *is* extremely important, so overlook this at your book's peril!

Social media

Social media is where anyone can be whatever they want to be, and it's true that many of the posts you'll see are filtered, cropped, and angled to perfection. But people on social media are also keenly attuned to nuances of authenticity on their preferred platforms. They know when they're being sold something. So while it's certainly the norm to use filters on Instagram or to only share the happiest of your life updates on Facebook, it's important to authentically use these spaces.

What does this even mean? To authentically use social media is to be part of these online communities with no ulterior motive. If you don't get on Instagram until your book is coming out, and then you only post about how people should order your book, people won't want to follow you. It will be clear you're only here for the sales.

Eighty-twenty is an excellent lean-to-fat ratio for a savory hamburger, for those of us who eat meat. This rule inspired the "eighty-twenty rule" of social media. Only twenty percent of your social media posting should be self-promotion; the other eighty percent needs to be genuine engagement with your community. For every one post you make publicizing your book, you should make four posts about your reading habits or your own life or share something that someone else has done.

You also can't take, take, take on social media (or anywhere in life) without ever giving. If you want people to like and comment on your posts, follow you, and pay attention when you post about your book, you have to do the same for others. This is how you build an authentic, excited online community that will be there when you need it.

Social media is not a place for competition. Those authors who are performing well on social media are not in competition with you. Rather, they are part of an online community you want to be part of as well. If you approach every interaction on social media with the mindset that you are engaging with and supporting your community, you'll be able to build your own niche community faster. Give freely, support others eagerly, and celebrate whatever you can. By gladly and freely supporting others on social media, you encourage them to do the same for you—though, always, reciprocation is not the point, but merely a bonus of engaging with your online communities.

Here is some advice about using some of the most popular social media platforms as an author. To learn more about getting reviews from other creators on these platforms, check out our section on Reviews (page 203).

Facebook

Facebook is still around, yes, and people still use it to connect with people and topics they care about. It's a good idea to be present on Facebook, even if this isn't where you put most of your social media energy. If someone searches for you on Facebook, you want to show up in the results. If you'd prefer for fans to follow you on Instagram or somewhere else, you can make sure your Facebook feed is primarily photos shared from your Instagram account to redirect visitors to your preferred platform(s).

Pages versus profiles

Lots of people have personal Facebook profiles, but those aren't the same as professional Facebook pages. If you're looking at a Facebook page and you're unsure if it's a professional page or a personal profile, the best way to figure it out is to see if you are prompted to "Add Friend" or "Like." Facebook invites you to "Add Friend" when you're looking at someone's personal profile; it asks you to "Like" a professional page.

If you want to be present on Facebook as an author, you'll need a professional Facebook page. Pages are always public, so anyone can go see them, and they have different features from a personal profile. Using your personal Facebook profile to promote your book and yourself as an author will seriously limit you in a lot of ways, which is why we so strongly recommend against it. Here are some ways in which professional Facebook pages are designed to help you pro-

FUN FACT

You can "follow" both Facebook profiles and pages. When you become someone's friend or like a business on Facebook, you automatically follow them, so you'll see their updates in your feed. You can "unfollow" a friend whose memes you don't want to see; you can also "unfollow" a creator or business if you want to support them by "liking" but don't wish to see their updates.

mote yourself and your book and engage with fans in a safe, appropriate way.

For starters, pages can tag other pages, but pages are not supposed to be allowed to tag personal profiles. That means that if your publisher or a book reviewer is talking about you on their Facebook page, they can't tag your personal profile. They can only tag you and connect with you there if you have a professional Facebook page.

FUN FACT

It's against Facebook policy to promote from a personal Facebook profile! While it's fine to share some of your bookish content to your personal profile, you'll want to start by posting it on your professional page.

Facebook pages offer the option to list merchandise in a shop by linking to other sellers, like Bookshop or Barnes and Noble. While Facebook shops don't drive a lot of sales to most merchandise, it's nice to be able to link to your book in every place where people can find you. You can also choose to direct these sales to wherever you want, so you can help out Bookshop and the local bookstores it supports, or you can link to your personal local independent bookstore, or you can link to your own website, if you sell your book yourself.

Facebook pages offer the option to have a "reviews" page, so people can review your books there if you enable this. Facebook pages can also have an "events" tab where you can share your upcoming author appearances to help drive traffic there. These are just a couple of the ways in which you can use the options on a Facebook page to manage your online author presence.

You may have noticed that most of these benefits are "options." That's one of the coolest parts about using a professional Facebook page. You can customize it in certain ways to best represent your brand and convey the information that's important to readers of your book. For example, an author wouldn't use the "hours" or "location" features on their Facebook page like a physical store might. Since you don't need these options, you can just omit them.

We're not going to list the specific instructions for creating a Facebook page, because Facebook changes in small ways all the time. By the time this book gets published, the process might be entirely different. But if you navigate to the "Pages" section of your Facebook account, you should be able to easily find the "Create New Page" button to get started, and then simply follow the prompts to launch your professional Facebook page.

If you need help getting your Facebook page started, try running a Google search for "create Facebook page" plus the current year. Choose the article with the most recent date. Adding the year when researching any technical issue is important to make sure you don't wind up reading through an obsolete guide from 2013!

Cover image

Creating a Facebook page cover image is an absolute nightmare. Just ask any designer who has ever tried to design a Facebook cover image graphic. The trouble is that your cover image has to look good on all kinds of devices: desktop computer screens, laptops, tablets, and phones. Its design has to be supremely flexible without looking stupid in its most radical dimensions.

You can Google the recommended dimensions for Facebook cover images. You should be looking for two recommended dimensions—the "desktop" dimension and the "mobile" dimension. Your cover image will need to look good as a super-wide desktop cover image as well as a short, stout mobile cover image. A good way to make this happen is to create a long image in the desktop image dimensions, but then concentrate all your crucial information or imagery in the center, where the mobile cover image dimensions lie.

PRO TIP

Don't forget to add the year with this search too!

If this sounds confusing to you, that's because this is confusing. Don't be afraid to watch a tutorial or even to tap in a professional designer friend who might be able to do this correctly more easily. Once you have a cover image uploaded, check it on as many different devices as you can, at least a desktop computer and a phone. Continue tweaking the image until it's right.

IMPORTANT NOTE

If you're lucky enough to have a friend who is a designer and wants to help you with tasks like this, it's crucially important not to take advantage. You must pay anyone who performs a service for you, whether they're a friend or not. If it feels weird to hand off money to a friend, pay them "in kind" by taking them out to dinner, babysitting their kids, or buying them a gift. Them saying, "That's not necessary!" is not an excuse. It is necessary. You must pay people for the labor they provide to you.

Invite your friends

When you first launch your professional Facebook page—or if you've already launched it but haven't taken this step yet—invite your friends and family to follow you. These people are supposed to support you; the least they can do is click one button to like you for free and boost your social media following.

You can invite all your Facebook friends to support your page, or you can limit your invitations to close friends and family. If you only invite certain people, it's a good idea to also share your professional Facebook page on your personal profile feed so your whole friends list has the opportunity to see it. You might be surprised who chooses to support you!

It's okay and sometimes way more effective to directly ask people to support you. Some of your friends may not use their Facebook accounts often, or may skip many of their notifications, so getting an individual text from you about it might be all they need to hop on and press "like"!

What to post

The cool thing about Facebook is that you can post pretty much anything, from memes to articles to promotions. It's also not incredibly important to post to your Facebook page every day or even regularly. Post to Facebook when it feels right and natural. Of course, you'll want to post all your bookish updates, from your cover reveal to your pre-order links to your release date celebration, and then beyond to reviews and events.

Just like most social networks, Facebook is a place for sharing other people's posts as well. Don't hesitate to share a relevant meme or post from another account to your professional page. Support other authors you know or enjoy by sharing their important book updates, and maybe they'll return the favor (though don't *expect* them to return the favor unless you have an explicit agreement!).

Hashtags

Some people use hashtags on Facebook, but they don't do much work there. While social platforms like Instagram and Twitter use hashtags to develop complex, niche online communities and make searching easy, Facebook does not. It's better to avoid using hashtags on Facebook and keep your posts clean and easy to understand.

"Like as your page"

You may be aware that you can like pages on Facebook. For example, you can "like" your favorite restaurant down the street, which means your personal Facebook profile will follow that restaurant's professional Facebook page. You'll see if they make any updates, and you'll be added to their follower list.

But you can also like pages from your professional Facebook page rather than from your personal Facebook profile. You may want to use your personal profile to like all the best happy hour spots around town, but maybe you want to use your professional page to like other authors and bookish organizations.

Go to the page you want to like from your professional page and find the "Like" button—but don't press it! Instead, click the three dots to the right, then find "Like as Your Page" on the drop-down list. If you run several professional Facebook pages (say, one for your yoga podcast, one for your mommies' group, and one for your author stuff), it'll let you choose which page to like from.

Events

Facebook is a great way to get your upcoming events in one place and make their details super accessible. Your Facebook page should have an "events" tab where all your upcoming events are posted in chronological order for fans to find. Below upcoming events, Facebook also keeps a log of past events so you or fans can reference those. Having lots of past events will also make you look more experienced and valuable for potential hosts of future events!

Sometimes the venue will create the Facebook event; in that case, you can ask them to make you a "co-host." You'll have to accept the co-host request on your end, and then their event should show up in your events tab. Be sure to review the details to make sure your information matches, and check that they have your name spelled correctly, your book title correct, and correct links and other information.

If you're doing a big, collaborative event like a conference or festival, there should certainly be a Facebook event created by the organizers. If these events feature more than just a handful of authors and vendors, the organizer will likely not want to make all those people co-hosts. In that case, you can simply share the event to your professional Facebook page and make it clear you will be there.

Some people even make sort of "sub-events" where they will

advertise their specific presence at a larger event. For example, perhaps your local library is hosting a book fair and thirty authors are invited. The library will probably make a Facebook event for the book fair. However, you could choose to make another event called "[Name] at the [Branch name] Library Book Fair" to invite your own network to, which will make it clear that you will be at the event and outline what you'll be doing there. If you choose to do this, be sure to link the official event page in your description.

If it's going to fall to you to make the Facebook event for your upcoming event, you can do this under the "events" tab of your page. Give the event a clear and concise name; this is not the place to be fancy and poetic. Make it very clear what the event is, even if the name feels a little boring. Be sure to double-check the date, time, and location so all your details are correct. Write a clear and detailed description for the event that will tell all potential attendees everything they need to know. Ask yourself what kind of information you might want to know if you were attending an event. Is it inside or outside? Is there a rain plan or rain date? Are tickets required? Can they be purchased at the door, ahead of time, or both? Is there a lot of walking involved? Is it wheelchair accessible? It's also a good idea to produce a nice graphic for the event's cover image, which you can do easily using a program like Canva.

No matter how you get your event up on Facebook, don't forget the most important step of the process: share it! Share that event to your professional page just often enough that it doesn't get annoying. If you're planning six months ahead, maybe post about it once or twice a month until the month beforehand. Definitely post about it at least weekly in the month leading up to the event; the week before the event, don't be afraid to post about it pretty much every day. Just be sure those posts are each a little different so your followers don't get sick of looking at the same thing over and over!

Instagram

Picture it: you have a beautiful Instagram page with tons of followers who simply cannot wait for your next book to come out. That's the dream, but how do we get there?

Instagram has a reputation for promoting fakeness and flattening complexity into banal snapshots. Yes, there are people on Instagram who make a living by being hot and using filters creatively. Yes, there are people on Instagram who are not what they say they are. Yes, there is a lot of room for toxic behavior on a social platform that is so focused on appearance. But we don't have to play the Instagram game; we can use it authentically and in a way that uplifts rather than compares.

Instagram is in some ways the simplest social media platform. You take a picture, and then you post it. You don't even need stellar text because the focus is on the image. (But *you* need good text, because you're a writer.) The platform is so simple that you have lots of room to develop your account and hone your brand there. Let's start by talking about the pictures themselves.

The pictures

Sure, anyone with a smartphone can snap a picture and pop it up on Instagram. But there's a lot more to it than that. Because just about everyone is walking around with professional-grade cameras in their pockets now, the quality of the average photo has skyrocketed. Gone are the days of blurry shots and thumbs covering the lens. When you can snap a hundred images in a few seconds and pick the one you like best, it's crucial that you're only posting quality images on Instagram.

Start by making sure you know how to use your equipment. If you feel like a stranger to your phone camera, ask someone who knows more than you or find a tutorial online to get a handle on the basics. Try snapping some different kinds of photos around your home to get the hang of it. Plants and books make great subjects. Pets and children are infamous for moving around a lot, so maybe start with something inanimate if you're a beginner and level up to trying to get a good picture of Max the malamute.

When you take a photo, make sure the lighting is good. Natural light tends to be best, and the light source should be facing your subject rather than behind it. Never use fluorescent lighting when you can avoid it, as it looks unnatural and can wash out your subject. If you're photographing a book, be careful to place the light somewhere it won't cast a glare across the cover.

PRO TIP

Lighting your object from the side or in other creative ways can be fun! But generally, proper lighting can go a long way in making amateur photos look professional.

Lay out your photo intentionally. This means that you don't just throw your book down and click from any odd angle; choose your backdrop, lay your book down, try a few different angles, and figure out what looks best. One of the biggest challenges with photographing books is that they're rectangular, so it's really obvious when the angle of the camera is slightly off. Most phone cameras have a "grid" option you can turn on so you can view your photo subjects through a grid to help center them and get your angles right. Do your best to photograph books face-on, so the lines are straight in every direction. If you take a slightly crooked photograph, you can always fix it later on your phone's photo editing tool, but the more you have to manipulate a photo, the more false it'll look.

PRO TIP

A great way to avoid all of this is to intentionally photograph books from fun angles. This can also help you avoid a glaring reflection from your light source.

Pretty accoutrements can be a great way to make a book photo jazzy. If you're not sure what this means, go onto Instagram and search #bookstagram, and you'll figure it out pretty quickly. But don't throw any random stuff into a picture just to make it busier. You have to choose your photo flair carefully so it will contribute to the whole image rather than taking it over or making it messy.

There's no good way to advise further about how or what to do with your Instagram photos in general. The best way to gain an understanding of Instagram photography is to follow people who are doing what you want to do and try to take inspiration from them. And the best way to hone your own skills is to start snapping.

Your profile

One unique thing about Instagram is it's easy to look at someone's Instagram presence as a whole. On Facebook or Twitter, a viewer can see a couple posts at a time, and they're likely going to be primarily text or links, so there's not a ton of visual cohesion there beyond the platform's own branding. But because a viewer can go to your Instagram profile and scroll through all your posts through the ages, it's worth considering what your images will look like all together.

Some people choose a theme for their Instagram profiles really specifically and with a lot of intention. They might only post pink photos, or only in black and white, or they might try to include the entire rainbow in every single picture. Some people might only post muted colors; lots of people post only in shades of white and beige. Some people might only post crisp architectural lines; others might only post organic matter like flowers and seashells.

You don't have to be this specific or intentional with your profile as a whole, but you can if you want to. Take a look and see what kind of vibe your profile is giving off. If your photos appear to be visually all over the place, you might want to consider homing in on a style and trying to make the feed look cleaner.

There are a lot of different ways to develop a more cohesive look on your Instagram profile. You can use the same background for all your pictures, like a white wall or a wooden table. You can take pictures of the same kinds of things, like books and cats only.

You can avoid posting non-photo images, like memes, and instead put those only in your Instagram story.

While you shouldn't worry too much about what your profile looks like as a whole if it's not super important to you, it is worth taking a look and seeing what kind of vibe your Instagram is giving off at a glance. If you want to try something new, find someone whose aesthetic you enjoy and see what you can do to emulate them.

PRO TIP

There's a huge difference between emulating and copying another social account. It's normal to like what someone else is doing and take inspiration when developing your own vibe. But you definitely don't want to copy someone closely. You don't want to be able to hold up the two images together and say, "This is the same picture."

Handles

Your social media handle is the username people can search for to find you. Usually formatted starting with an "at symbol" like @wildlingpress, your handle is different from your display name. Often, both your handle and your display name will show up when you post. However, of course, each social media platform handles handles differently.

When you reserve a handle, other people can't then use it as long as your account is active. That's a big reason to claim your handle on Instagram and other social media platforms. Having a handle also helps other people to find you more easily by navigating directly to your unique handle rather than having to search your name and comb through the results.

Your handle should be 1. related to you or your brand and 2. consistent across platforms. Both of these recommendations are for the purpose of making you easy for your fans to find online. It also helps to make your handle relatively simple, something you could say to someone in passing that they might remember.

In theory, the best handle is your name, and in theory, you'd be able to get @yourname on every social media platform you wish to be on. But we're in the future, and the internet has been around for a long time now. So the odds are good that even if you have a fairly unique name—like, oh, Christina Kann, as a random example—you still won't be able to get that handle. (Follow me @ christinakann_.)

Your handle might be related to your brand, if you can make that work reasonably and attractively. (As in, do not follow me @indiebookpublishingfromstarttofinish_itsgoingtobeawesome). Maybe you write poetry and your handle is @poetrybycate (which is probably already taken). Maybe you write romance and your handle is @kisstina (which is probably already taken).

As I've mentioned I think at least once, the handle you want is probably already taken. So do your best to get the handle that makes sense for you, and then commit. You don't want to change your handle after you've been marketing it for years. Your handle will become part of your brand, and you want it to be consistent and clear.

Instagram is the only social media platform that exclusively shows your handle when you post and not your display name. In order to view your display name, users must navigate to your profile. Because of this, it's important to make sure your Instagram handle is clear, memorable, and consistent.

Hashtags

Unlike Facebook, Instagram makes great use of hashtags, and you will want to harness their power when you post on this platform. Instagram users use hashtags in a lot of different ways, but it all comes down to organizing their interests. If someone is thinking they might want to get a tattoo of an owl, they can look up #owltattoo to get some inspiration. An expectant parent might look up #parentingtips or #newparent to connect with other people who are going through a similar experience. Booklovers might look up a hashtag of the name of the book they're currently reading, like #thehateugive, to see other opinions or engage with other readers about it, or they might more generally look up #currentlyreading to see what other booklovers are up to.

On Instagram, users can also follow hashtags the way they would follow an account. This is sort of like joining a chat room for a specific interest; the user is saying they're interested in seeing all content of this particular subject matter, no matter who publishes it. Booklovers can follow hashtags like #indieauthor, #weneeddiversebooks, #amreading, or #bookstagram so they regularly see book-related posts from all kinds of accounts beyond the ones they are explicitly following.

Where do hashtags go? Most people put their hashtags in the image caption section after their caption as a bulk group. While some may not like how this looks, lots of people do it, so it's commonly accepted. Besides this, most posts won't show those hashtags that come after the caption, as the caption is cut off after about ten words with an ellipsis one must click on to read more. You can also drop down a couple lines to include your hashtags below; however, each line must include a period or another punctuation mark or an emoji, as Instagram automatically collapses line breaks that are completely empty.

Some people prefer to add their hashtags as the first comment under their picture after it has been posted. This is often an aesthetic choice to present a cleaner caption compared to the route recommended in the previous paragraph. However, Instagram has stated that hashtags belong in post captions, not in their comments, and those included in comments get overlooked by Instagram's algorithm. So play it safe and post your hashtags in the captions.

You can also include your hashtag in your caption text when it makes sense. For example, you could post, "Happy to finally be at the #FestivalOfTheBook!" along with a photo you've snapped upon arriving at this event. You could post, "What's everyone working on today? Today I #AmWriting," knowing that #amwriting is a common hashtag authors use to connect with each other. However, be careful to avoid overusing hashtags in your captions, as well as avoid using generic hashtags that won't get you anywhere. A caption like, "So #grateful to be #working with such an amazing #team!" is not only hard to read; it's not getting any targeted audience to that post. People who are looking up #grateful are probably not readers on the prowl for their next book.

An Instagram post caption can include up to thirty hashtags, and many people include that number to ensure their post shows up in as many searches as possible. However, the Instagram algorithm (more on Page 192) has been known to suppress posts with that many hashtags, giving preference to posts with five to ten hashtags. Use your hashtags wisely, ensuring that each packs a valuable punch.

PRO TIP

People with visual impairments and other disabilities may use a text-to-speech tool to view their social media feeds. This means an AI program does its best to read the text it comes across to the user. A hashtag with all lowercase letters looks like nonsense to an AI reader. However, if you capitalize the first letter of each word in a hashtag, including words you typically wouldn't like "a" and "the," the AI reader can see that it's looking at one unit consisting of several different words, and it can read the hashtag more intuitively to the user.

The social platform formerly known as Twitter

Twitter is sort of the lawless wasteland of the internet—even more so now that it's owned by Elon Musk. Twitter is independent, for better or for worse, whereas Facebook and Instagram are both owned by Meta. Twitter censors its users less, allowing more taboo language and suggestive images. And, perhaps most importantly, it can be really hard for people to grasp what they're supposed to do on Twitter.

From Twitter's founding in 2006 until 2017, the platform only allowed 140 characters per tweet. Now Twitter allows its users to post a whopping 280 characters per tweet. For comparison, there are 280 characters between the beginning of this paragraph and the end of this sentence. So Twitter is primed for shooting off brief, concise thoughts and updates in as few words as possible.

If you're ever home alone or working out and you have a mildly funny thought and you wish you had someone to say it to, you can tweet that. If you have a writing update or gripe, you can tweet that. If you have a cover reveal or a link to pre-order your book, you can tweet that. You can tweet just about anything, as long as it's 280 characters or less.

HORRIBLE FACT

Under Elon Musk's ownership, Twitter has indeed been rolling back censorship of its users. It now also censors its hate less! In April 2023, Twitter removed language protecting trans people in particular and marginalized groups in general from hate speech on its platform. Wildling no longer uses Twitter because that would conflict with our mission to uplift and protect marginalized voices. However, many people still use Twitter, and you should decide for yourself if it's right for you.

It's also worth noting that tweets can't be edited like Facebook or Instagram posts can. Once you send a tweet, it's set in stone. If you want to change something about a tweet, you must delete the original and then tweet the updated language. Alternatively, you could simply comment on your original tweet correcting yourself.

Or, on the flip side, you could just let the error go, depending on its gravity.

The issue comes with understanding what will land with your audience on Twitter. Twitter is vast, wild, and fickle. Odd things trend and it can be hard to figure out why. The platform shows you tweets from people you follow, but also tweets that people you follow have interacted with, and also tweets that you might just like for some reason. So who are you talking to? And what should you say?

Twitter is *not* the place for tons of overt book promotion. People will tire of seeing it and have no cause to follow you. Typically, people engage with tweets that are funny or relatable, preferably both. That's why tweeting any odd thought that passes through your brain and makes you giggle to yourself is a good place to start. Other people have probably had this same thought or can relate to what you're saying.

The best way to figure out Twitter is to—shocker—hang out on Twitter and see what other people are doing. Follow some independent authors and see what they're doing, what works for them. Then emulate—never copy!—their strategy.

Handles

Twitter requires handles and display names, and when you tweet, it displays both along with your tweet. Often, users retain one consistent handle while changing their display name to reflect something current about themselves or perhaps a joke or even a bit of a status update. Authors who are using Twitter professionally should probably not be changing their display name often or incorporating unrelated jokes, but they might add "is writing" or "is querying" to their display name, as in "Christina Kann is writing" or "Christina Kann, indie author," to indicate what they're working on.

Retweeting

Retweeting is the easiest way to tweet to your profile. Someone else has said something you find funny or relate to, and you repost their tweet. Their handle remains with the post after you retweet it, so it's clear to everyone that this person has authored the tweet and you have merely retweeted it. However, this low-stakes, low-effort method can be a great way to get started on Twitter, to get a hold of your Twitter voice, or even to engage a bit on a day when you don't have much spare energy or time.

Threads

Sometimes people have more than 280 characters' worth of stuff to say, and that's understandable. If you find yourself needing to post something a bit longer on Twitter, and you're certain you can't cut it down, you can create a tweet thread. Alternatively, perhaps you want to post a list of something, like your favorite local bookstores with a brief shoutout for each, which would lend itself to the thread format, as each list item could have its own tweet in the thread.

To create a thread, make the first tweet, then open the tweet and look for the "add another tweet" button at the bottom. When you post the second tweet, you'll see that it's attached to the first.

Some Twitter users opt to number their tweet threads like page numbers, ending the first with "1/X" (X being the number of tweets they plan to post) or perhaps "1/" if they're unsure how many tweets they plan to post to indicate that this is the first in a series of indeterminate number.

YouTube

If you already know how to edit video content or know someone you could hire to edit your videos, YouTube might be a good platform for you. Or if you're interested in hiring someone to regularly produce videos for you, YouTube might work for you. Video editing is a really useful skill, and if you're eager to learn how to do it, you should do it. But for those who don't have editing budgets and aren't keen on editing videos, YouTube is probably not the right platform to start with.

YouTube content can be so many different things. It can be short (just a couple of seconds) or long (longer than a feature film, if your account is verified, or up to fifteen minutes if it's not). It can be simple (you speaking to the camera) or complex (an expertly produced presentation of video, voiceover, music, animation, etc.). It can be live action or animated. It can be silly, informative, or just plain stupid.

Authors who are considering starting a YouTube channel should ask themselves what they might post about. You could post book reviews, which would probably be a safe place to start if you're just dipping your toes into video. Book review videos can be short and simple, just you holding the book in question and talking to the camera about your thoughts. You could also post the grammatical or editorial tips you're learning during your book production process.

People love to get a behind-the-scenes look at the artists they love. Perhaps you could share videos of important, physical (ie. not happening on a computer) moments of your book production process, like unboxing your printer's proof or signing copies for the local bookstore.

YouTube is geriatric in terms of social media platforms, having been founded in 2005, and it tends to see more users than other platforms. Because of this, there is a huge wealth of content to be perused. The flip side is that it's harder than ever to make original content there and get noticed. If you're not sure where to get started, get watching. Find some YouTubers who post about bookish things—or content related to your book's subject matter—and take note of what they do. Being inspired (not copying, but emulating) is a great place to start developing your own YouTube content strategy.

TikTok

TikTok is another video platform, but unlike YouTube, you don't need specialized knowledge to produce TikToks. The TikTok app includes features to film and edit your video easily, as well as transcribe captions and add accoutrements like stickers and images. Anyone with smartphone fluency could hop on TikTok and be producing their videos comfortably within an hour or so.

That's not to say that TikTok is perfect or easy. The controls can be a bit finicky, but that's always going to be a problem when you're editing content using only your thumbs. Beyond that, producing TikToks can be hard. You can record something you feel is worthwhile, but after editing that content, listening to yourself say the same thing over and over, it can be hard to sustain the feeling that it's worth posting. It's hard to think you're clever enough! It's extremely challenging and vulnerable to post content that involves your own face and/or voice.

But the thing is, tons of people do it, and so can you—if it's something you're interested in pursuing. Plenty of people simply lurk on Tiktok watching other people's videos, and that's perfectly acceptable. But if you're interested in posting on TikTok, you can totally strengthen your skills and your self-esteem to make it happen.

You may have read this line before in the previous sections, but . . . the best way to learn how to post on TikTok is to hang out on TikTok and take note of videos you enjoy. See what content other people are posting in what ways, and figure out where you might fit into the feed. Do you have anything to add to the conversation? Are their video concepts inspiring any of your own?

As you'll probably notice quickly, most TikToks are *fast*, a holdover from when the app was originally developed in 2016 and the videos could be no longer than fifteen seconds. Today, TikTok videos can run up to *ten minutes*, and yet many retain their snappy pace and smash-cuts.

When you're feeling ready, try recording a TikTok of your own. Consider starting by reproducing a TikTok trend you've seen going around, so you can easily figure out what to say and do. As for the rest of TikTok, you'll have to figure it out on your own by bopping around the app and seeing what's up. Just be warned: TikTok can be a hypnotizing vortex of content! You may want to consider setting a time limit for the app on your phone's settings if you start to feel the pull of the void.

Cyberbullying

While social media can provide a loving, mutual, supportive community for many authors, it also brings the rest of the world right into the palm of your hand. Some of these people have different opinions than you—and worse, some of these people just want to cause harm. Cyberbullying is a very real thing, and popular authors have been bullied off social media platforms before. You've surely seen it yourself if you hang out in online spaces. It's important to be ready should online abuse ever come your way.

If you put yourself out there in online spaces—which you should, to build your author network—there is a very real chance that someone will at some point come after you for your writing, your ideas, or even your identity. If you feel like you're being antagonized online, take a moment to ask yourself: *Are they being abusive? Or do they just have a different opinion from me?*

If someone comes to you online in bad faith to have a public argument about a controversial topic, move carefully. Don't engage in a lengthy back-and-forth; show respect and compassion; keep your cool. Don't presume to speak about things you don't know about, including other people's identities. Be firm about the things you're sure about, like your values and your own identity.

As we are all aware, a social media snafu can ruin a person's career. Always conduct yourself with dignity in online spaces and commit to being the bigger person when other people are showing their asses.

More on handles

Social media handles can be so frustrating (not to imply that the author has ever struggled with her own social media handles). Nearly every social media platform requires you to have a handle, yet they each have different requirements. Twitter doesn't allow periods in your handle, nor short nor long handles, whereas Instagram and Twitter both allow underscores, and TikTok permits both except no periods at the ends.

platform	underscores	periods	characters
Instagram	• yes	• yes	• up to 30
Twitter	• yes	• no	• 4-15
TikTok	• yes	• yes except at the end	• up to 24

If you're lucky, you can nab @yourname across all platforms. It helps to have a unique name, but uniqueness isn't necessarily enough (again, not that the author has been struggling with this AT ALL). The odds are good that your first-choice handle has already been claimed by someone else with your name or a name adjacent to yours. This sucks; it really does. But you have to pivot and try new options until you find the one that works. Maybe you can add "author" at the end of your name, or "writes." Numbers, especially multi-digit numbers, aren't recommended as they're harder to remember.

Ideally, you'll want to have the same handle across all social media platforms. That way, you can tell people, "Find me online @yourname," rather than give them a bulleted list. It looks neat on promotional materials, and it's easier to remember if you have to share with someone verbally. If you can't get identical handles across the board, aim for similar. You don't want one account to have some seemingly unrelated handle and people to question if it's you.

There are a couple techniques you can try to help you develop your social media handles. Start by exploring your name and all its variations. Think about what you do and who you are—"author," "writer," "books," "creator"—and consider variations of those words. Run some keywords through a word associations generator to explore some similar alternatives. Ask your friends, family, and colleagues for input or ideas. Let all that simmer until one of those handles clicks.

"The algorithm"

Sure, we've all heard of the dreaded algorithm, but what is it? "The algorithm" is any of the elaborate computer code that social media platforms develop to process all their content. The algorithm decides what posts to show which people when based on a whole plethora of their personal data. The algorithm of each social platform shows you the content it thinks you want based on how you've been engaging with that platform recently.

The algorithm isn't a stagnant system. It's changing every day as developers strengthen it and users continue inputting data. To some, trying to beat the algorithm seems like a futile task. You hear other platform users talk about "the algorithm" and its preferences, and yet it's hard to know what's true and what's not.

Because you can't rely on myths about the algorithm, it's important to consistently review your own data across all your social media platforms to see what's working and what's not. All of these platforms keep track of your reach and growth for you. This tracking is called "Insights" on Instagram; on TikTok, you go to "Creator tools" and then "Analytics"; on Twitter, you can click the small insights graphic button under any of your own tweets or view more detailed data at analytics. twitter.com.

FUN FACT

On Instagram, you need a "business account" to see Insights. But it's really easy to switch to a business account in your account settings. After all, your author brand is your business!

Scheduling social media posts

Social media can be time consuming. It's hard to take time every day to strategize and write and/or photograph and/or film and edit social media posts across all platforms. What you can do instead is sign up for a social media scheduling program like Buffer or Hootsuite and get all your posting done in bunches. Or you can make use of various social media platforms' built-in scheduling features.

You can photograph all your Instagram posts for a month in an hour or two by walking around your home or neighborhood and snapping pictures of your beautiful book. Then you can go home and upload them into your scheduling program and pump out a couple of excellent captions (you're a writer, after all) and then be done with it for the month, or week, or however long you've scheduled for. You can draft snappy tweets as they come to you and schedule promotions posts to Facebook ahead of time.

Using a scheduling program doesn't mean you'll never hang out live on the app. You should still spend at least a couple of moments every day or so on your social platforms connecting with your community, responding to comments, and uplifting others. When you schedule your posts ahead of time, you reserve more of your daily energy for making authentic connections on social media.

Final thoughts about social media

Social media is vast, varied, and very complicated. It changes constantly. By the time you read this, some details mentioned here might already be outdated. This book's first draft lauded Twitter as a wonderful independent platform and was subsequently revised to reflect Elon Musk's ownership. Maybe you're reading this after Musk has relinquished the platform and it's now thriving without him. Maybe you're reading this after Twitter has collapsed entirely.

With everything in life, and with social media in particular in the context of this book, you must do your own research and arrive at your own understandings. There is rarely a right answer, and what seems right today might be clearly wrong tomorrow. Stay flexible, pivot when you need to, and rely on your community and yourself to navigate the murky waters

Your brand

Branding is a concept typically reserved for businesses, right? Well, writing is your business now, and therefore your actual personality, your author persona, and your book(s) should meld together into your brand.

Your brand isn't aspirational or out of reach. It doesn't mean setting a goal for yourself and hoping you get there. Branding isn't inauthentic or contrived. Branding simply means being mindful of what content you're presenting, why you're presenting it, how you can best present it, and how that connects to who you are as a person.

When you're trying to figure out your brand, take a realistic look at yourself first. What are you into? Books, computers, cats, coffee, red wine, rain? What kind of person are you? Writer, parent, ENFP, Aquarius, half-elf rogue, manager, runner, poet? What are your values, your priorities? Friendship, fitness, literature, honesty, beauty, justice? How do you like to express yourself? Flowery, constant, straightforward, quiet, loud, laughing, serious? All these things together make up your brand. Your brand is all the cool things that are important to you, presented in a way that makes you relatable and interesting to other people.

What do you do with your brand? Well, for the most part, you just keep it in mind. When you're about to post on social media, ask yourself, "Does this match my brand?" and if not, "Why do I want to post this?" You could ultimately post it or not; the point is that you consider your brand when you're producing content and consider altering content that doesn't match your brand.

Connecting with other people to market your book

Stay organized

Marketing your book is complicated and takes a long time and involves lots of tiny little pieces coming together. You can't embark on a project like this without having some way to stay organized.

It's tempting to say, "Whatever organizational system works for you, do that." But if that system isn't a spreadsheet, it's hard to fathom how you're going to keep it all straight. Google Sheets, Microsoft Excel, Apple Numbers—all these programs are designed to help you keep track of vast projects with complex moving pieces.

Make yourself a publicity spreadsheet. Organize *that* with whatever system works for you. But since most of your publicity outreach is going to start on the computer, it makes sense that you'd have one spreadsheet where you keep track of it all, and when you complete a task, you can simply bop on over to your publicity spreadsheet and take note of it. You can add links and set reminders for yourself to follow up at a certain time.

Keeping a spreadsheet record of all your publicity efforts will change your book promotion game. Do yourself a favor and start with creating that spreadsheet. Dump in all of the publicity ideas you've been collecting ever since you decided you wanted to write a book. Then you'll have all your tasks in one place, and you can start to organize and prioritize them. Make one tab for BookTokers you hope to connect with and another tab for keeping track of your personal network, another for local media, another for Bookstagrammers. Looking at the pretty spreadsheet all empty and clean will hopefully motivate you to dive right into promoting your book! It will also help you figure out where to start.

Your network

Start your marketing efforts with your personal network. Your personal network is your family, friends, colleagues, neighbors, and anyone else who knows you and would have a personal investment in supporting you. These people should want to support you. Your close friends and family may be keen to tell the world about your book and support you by attending every author event. Acquaintances may be happy to support your book by purchasing a copy or signing up for your email newsletter.

You can also activate specific people in your personal network for specific purposes to support your book. For example, if your dad has a massive LinkedIn network, you can ask them to share your book release post with their connections. (Thanks, Dad!) If your college friend is now a fashion influencer on Instagram, reach out and ask them if they'd mind sharing your book posts on their story.

Often, intentionally asking individuals to do one or two meaningful tasks can be better than posting on social media asking for anyone to support you. People's eyes can slide right past your tweet announcement about pre-orders being open, but if you reach out to them directly, they're more likely to rise to the occasion and choose to support you.

Think creatively of people you didn't consider on your first brainstorm. What about your neighbor's sister who comes to barbecue in their backyard every week or two and chats with you about her job as a librarian? Do they want to buy copies of your book? Would they be open to talking about doing an author event there? What about your old college professor you've stayed connected with on Facebook? Does their class need to read this book, or could they recommend it to their students for additional reading?

After you've explored your entire network and made the most of its strengths, it's time to start reaching out to people outside of your personal network.

How to reach out

We're about to get into what kinds of media you can reach out to about your book, but before we even get there, let's talk about *how* to reach out to people about your book, whether you know them in real life, kind of know them on the internet, or have never met or spoken with them before.

Where to reach out

Start by reaching out to people in the way that's most natural to the relationship. For example, if you're reaching out to a friend of your grandma's who runs the local newspaper, ask her how you should contact him. If you're reaching out to an influencer you follow on Instagram, send them a direct message on Instagram. If you always go into your local bookstore and the sellers there know you, march your butt right on inside.

If you're not sure where to start, low-key online messages are the best for most people. See if you can find their email on their website or their social media bio. If not, send them a DM.

What to say

This is again dependent on the relationship. If you're reaching out to your high school best friend who now has a momfluencer blog to ask her to review your new picture book, sure, pour your heart out. But if you're reaching out to someone you don't know very well, here are some tips.

<u>Be brief</u>

Don't waste someone's time. A long message might not even get read if it seems like a lot to the recipient. Say all that you need to say in as few words as possible.

<u>Say how you know them</u>

And make it convincing. Don't just say, "I love your YouTube channel." No, you loved that one moment two videos ago when they played that word game. It made you laugh so much. If you follow them online, tell them why. Tell them how that relates to you.

If you're not familiar with them or their content, can you become so quickly? Can you listen to their most recent couple podcast episodes? Can you scroll through their feed from the past month or so? Can you read reviews of their book? Can you watch someone else interview them?

If you're not familiar with their work and can't get familiar quickly, be honest. Say, "I just discovered you/your show and I am so intrigued by X! I can't wait to catch up on the backlog/see what you post in the future."

Tell them who you are

Assume they don't know, because they probably don't. Tell them who you are, and more important, who you are *to them*. Tell them what you do, what you've written. If you're from the same town, mention it. If you went to the same college, mention it. If you're just getting started, say that. Tell them you're working on building connections.

Along with this, tell them about your book. If you're asking them to cover your book, they need to know what it is. What genre is it? How long is it? When does it come out? What's the short synopsis? What are the vibes? How is it connected to their branding?

Tell them what you want

Are you asking for a review, feature, or interview (more on those coming up next)? Are you asking them to do something they already do, or are you asking them to do something new? If you're asking them to do something new, why should they? Tell them what you want from them, and be specific. If you're not asking a straightforward question, how can you expect them to answer?

<u>Ask for their input, thank them, and send</u>

At the end, it's a good idea to say, "I'm happy to work to-gether however makes sense to you," or, "Interested to hear if you have any other ideas!" This will give them the opportunity to weigh in if they have a better idea than what you suggested. This will also protect you if you've perhaps asked for more than they can do at this time, like if you asked them to interview you, but their schedule is full, so they offer to do a feature announcing your book release.

Thank them. Duh.

PROOFREAD THE MESSAGE! You don't want to embar-rass yourself on a first impression by failing to catch a typo. Es-pecially if you're asking someone to respect you as a writer and possibly even attach their name to bolstering your writing career, you want that message to be flawless.

And send.

And write it down in your log.

And wait.

Reviews, features, and interviews

When people think about book publicity, they're likely think-ing about a review, a feature, or an interview. These are the three big ways book reviewers and other media can cover you and your book. When you're first contacting a book journalist or creator, try to see which path they're more familiar with or more interested in conducting for you. All three are great avenues that will put you and your book in front of a new audience.

What's a review?

A book review is when a reviewer receives a copy of your book (often for free), reads it, and then writes a blurb about their thoughts. A review may involve a rating out of five stars, but it doesn't have to. A review may involve notes about the book's conformation to its genre or its appropriateness for the target age group, but it doesn't have to. A review may involve the reviewer's likes and dislikes, but sometimes a review just looks like a rewrite of your book's synopsis with "great read" or some other pithy, empty compliment at the end. A book review can involve many things, but it's usually to some extent one reviewer's emotional and intellectual response to their experience of reading your book.

What's a feature?

A feature is when a reviewer or another journalist or influencer covers your book but has perhaps not read it and refrains from making review-type commentary on it. An Instagram influencer may not have time to read your book, but due to its content or their connection to you or just because they're nice, they're willing to share a post about your book to their story. Or perhaps your local newspaper doesn't often do book reviews and doesn't have anyone to fill that role, but they're happy to post an announcement when your book releases, as that constitutes local news. A feature is when any publication or creator posts about your book in a way that is not a review and not an interview.

What's an interview?

Naturally, an interview is a kind of article or post a publication or creator might produce in which they have interviewed you. They might interview you over Zoom and then post the video to YouTube; they might transcribe the interview and post that transcription to their blog. They might interview you live on Instagram Live or create a TikTok in which they're interviewing you in person. They might interview you over the phone and air it live on their radio station. They might interview you over Zoom for their podcast and post the recorded audio as a podcast episode.

Big publications

There are some notable publications you can submit your book to for review or feature. Many of these opportunities are paid, but some aren't. The bigger the publication, the more submissions they get, and the less likely it is that they'll select your book. So it's important to seek reviews and features from both big-name and smaller, independent reviewers. Here are some of the bigger ones you might want to explore:

- Kirkus (free review consideration or paid guaranteed review)
- Publisher's Weekly (free review consideration)
- Library Journal or School Library Jounal (free review consideration)
- Indies Today (paid guaranteed review)

Most bigger review publications don't permit follow-ups, and likely none of them permit phone calls, so be sure to find their review policy before reaching out. If you have trouble catching the attention of these high-volume book reviewers, try turning to some smaller, independent book reviewers.

Independent publications

Independent book publications and influencers can be found on Instagram (#bookstagram), TikTok (#booktok), Twitter, YouTube, podcasts, personal blogs, organizational blogs, and more. Indie reviewers might have a hundred Instagram followers or twelve thousand email newsletter subscribers. They might only review certain genres (#ireadya) or authors of certain identities (#blackbookstagram). They might only review books they can read along with their kids or their class. Independent reviewers come in all shapes and sizes, and it's up to you to see who matches your branding and seems like they might be willing to read and write a review about your book.

It's a good idea to both "shoot for the stars" and have some "sure bets" when it comes to reaching out to independent book reviewers, a concept we talked about back when we were looking for book endorsements. Endorsements and reviews are pretty much the same kind of content, after all; endorsements are reviews before your book is published, and reviews are endorsements after your book is published.

You would probably be safe reaching out to a small Bookstagrammer you've been connecting with for a long time over Instagram. They may only have two hundred followers, but they're extremely nice, and they have a book coming out soon, so maybe you can swap reviews. Even if their audience is small, they've demonstrated to you that they engage passionately with their community, so your book would be in good hands should they want and have time to review your book.

But you also want to reach out to reviewers who have thousands of followers and could possibly expose your book to a vast new audience. Because these reviewers have bigger followings, they receive more review requests simply because more people know they exist. Try starting with someone you've been following and engaging with for a long time; hopefully they'll recognize your handle and be willing to help.

Some indie reviewers have their submission requirements posted clearly on their website or social media account. "Please email myname@email.com with review submissions!" or, "Feel free to DM with review inquiries." You might also see, "Closed to submissions until June," or, "Currently closed to submissions." These sorts of messages indicate that the reviewer is taking a personal break from reviewing, or they've had so many review requests recently they can't possibly get through all they've committed to unless they take a break from receiving new submissions. Some indie reviewers might have their submission requirements posted on a page of their website or in a pinned post on their social media account. Whatever information they provide, be sure to follow their directions carefully.

There are many more independent reviewers than there are longstanding, prestigious bigger reviewers, and because of this, those independent reviewers get fewer requests. That's not to say that independent reviewers don't get a *lot* of book review requests; many of them get plenty. The odds are better for you in terms of getting noticed by an independent reviewer, but you still have to follow their rules and stand out.

Always keep in mind that independent book reviewers are often just one person or maybe occasionally two or three people working together to review books just for the sake of reviewing. If they don't answer you within a couple of weeks, it's okay to follow up (unless they state on their account or website that they don't permit follow-ups). Always be kind and understanding. If they don't have time for your book, that's not a reflection on you, and you must graciously accept their decision not to review your book and leave them alone.

FUN FACT

Some independent book reviewers offer paid review options, and a small portion may *only* offer paid review options, but for the most part, they offer honest reviews in exchange for a free copy of the book.

Some reviewers "only post positive reviews." This means that if they agree to review your book, but end up not enjoying it, they will not post a review of your book. The majority of reviewers, however, post "honest reviews." This means they'll be honest in their post about what they think of your book, for better or for worse. This is a risk you take when you ask people you don't personally know to review your book. They don't owe you a false opinion or genuine approval. If they don't like your book, there is nothing you can do to change that. However, you can limit the risk of getting a bad review by doing a bit of research first. What kinds of reviews have they done in the past? What have they disliked? Does your book feature something they've complained about in the past? If so, maybe they're not the reviewer for you.

If someone posts a negative review of your book, you must not defend yourself unless they've simply gotten something factually wrong. Don't shame that person or message them to tell them what you think. You simply refrain from reposting that review or otherwise telling your network about it. You accept the opinion quietly and move on, hoping the next reviewer will enjoy your book more. Nobody is obligated to enjoy any book, even if you think it's good. Almost forty thousand Goodreads users have granted a mere one-star rating to *Frankenstein* by Mary Wollstonecraft Shelley, one of the most beloved science fiction books of all time that's credited with launching the genre. No one is obligated to enjoy your book; however, you are obligated to be professional and courteous.

Traditional news media

"Traditional news media" is newspapers, magazines, and radio—the kind of media that wouldn't make your grandma nervous. For an independent author, particularly a debut indie author, the odds are strong that the *New York Times* isn't going to be interested in posting a review of your book. It's a good idea to start by contacting your local newspaper(s), community magazine(s), and relevant radio show(s).

Newspaper and radio station websites can be incredibly complex and confusing, as these types of media have tons of content coming in and out all the time. But do your best to find the publication or station's staff directory or contact page so you have a starting point for getting in touch with the right person.

Print media

At a newspaper or magazine, you're going to want to reach out to the person who is most likely to write about books. Some publications (and fewer every day) have designated book editors who are tasked exclusively with covering book reviews and book news. More commonly, a publication won't have a books editor, but they have an arts editor, or an arts and entertainment editor, who covers books, music, movies, theater, and more. Some publications may not have editors who specialize, but rather a team of features editors. If you can't find a books editor, contact the arts editor, and if you can't find an arts editor, reach out to a features editor.

Some publications will have a website page where they simply list their entire staff along with each person's position and contact information. A lot of the time, news media staff members want to be easily accessible to the public, as they are constantly looking for new stories and perspectives. But some websites may only provide email addresses without telling you what each person does. In that case, you'll have to browse around the publication or its website to see which writers are credited as having written book-related stories. Some publications may not have their staff contact information listed at all, and you'll have to figure out the right person to reach out to and attempt to access them through direct message on social media or a contact form on their personal website. This work is kind of like detective work, figuring out the best way to get your book in the limelight and then trying to find the person who can help you achieve that.

Radio

If you're interested in getting on the radio to talk about your book, you'll want to do some research and figure out what radio shows in your area would care about a book release. Radio stations change throughout the day, rotating radio shows by different hosts about different subjects, each show typically lasting an hour or two. Many radio shows are reserved exclusively for music, like, "The Lunchbox throwback jams. No ads for an hour over your lunch break!" But there are plenty of radio shows that revolve around conversations, like morning commute talk shows or smaller shows at odd hours.

Find the show that would cover your book. If your book is historical fiction, that evening talk show where three twenty-some-things give relationship advice to callers is *not* the show for you. Look for a radio show that covers local news, local art, history, books, or some other subject you can connect to your book.

Then, reach out directly to that show's host or organizer. Reaching out to the radio station at large will likely not get you where you need to go, as any given radio station is coordinating a dozen or more radio shows at once. But if you reach out directly to the host or manager of a specific show, you're much more likely to snag their interest and get to the next step of talking more about what an interview on their show might look like for you.

In all instances, avoid hello@, info@, or contact@ email addresses. There's no way to know who runs those inboxes or who will end up reviewing your email. If you can find literally any individual person to reach out to, reach out to them rather than emailing a generic email. If you can only find contact information for a person who you're pretty sure is not the right person, ask if they can help direct you to the appropriate contact.

Podcasts

Podcasts are not quite social media and definitely not traditional media, so they've earned their own section. If you've never really listened to the actual radio before, perhaps podcasts are more your speed. Podcasts are the radio shows of the future, automatically delivered to listeners' cell phones for them to listen to at their leisure. How can you get in those people's pockets? You need to guest on podcasts.

There are a ton of podcasts out there about all sorts of subjects, and plenty of redundancy there as well. There are hundreds of book-related podcasts, and beyond that, there are also podcasts about the niche subject of your book. And beyond that, there are plenty of podcasts that just interview people who have done cool stuff, regardless of what that is. All of these kinds of podcasts could be a good place to promote your book.

A good place to start is by listening to podcasts. Browse around for shows that seem to match the subject matter of your book. If you've written a young adult science fiction book, look for podcasts that focus on or even just occasionally cover YA literature and/or science fiction. If you've written a nonfiction history book, a history podcast that specializes in or even just sometimes touches on your subject will be a good avenue for you.

Ask for advice from your personal network. Let people know you're looking for podcasts that would suit your book, podcasts that at least occasionally interview guests, and see if they have any recommendations. Keep a list somewhere so you can sample some episodes from each podcast you're interested in before reaching out.

Some podcasts have forms on their website where you can apply to be a guest. A lot of podcasts don't, and you'll have to look for an email address or DM them on social media. As always, you'll want to keep your initial pitches short and sweet, thanking the creator for their work, explaining how your work ties into theirs, and asking if they might be interested in having you on the show.

Events

Participating in author events is probably the most labor-intensive way of promoting your book, but its payoff can be incredible. Events allow you to connect directly with your audience in real time. Events may be online or in person, short or long, a one-off or part of a larger event, but they all involve connecting with your community. For some authors, that feeling can be incredible.

For those authors who hesitate to seek out the company of so many people, start small at your local bookstore. You could even start out doing a book reading for friends and family at your own home to test the waters. See if you can talk yourself into leveling up to larger events as you go on. With each event you attend, your on-the-spot, in-person skills will strengthen, and your public author persona will develop.

Types of events

Signings

Book signings are in some ways the easiest sort of author event. Because of this, they tend to result in fewer sales compared to other kinds of events. Typically, a bookstore or another venue will allow an author to set up a table and readers may meet you and purchase a signed copy—if they wish. A bookstore will sell these copies on behalf of the author; if you're at another venue, especially a non-retail venue like a park, you may have to sell your own copies. Learn more about selling your own books on Page 223.

Book signings are so passive that it can be easy for readers to ignore them. For example, let's say you're doing a book signing at Barnes and Noble. Someone enters Barnes and Noble; they've come to buy the latest celebrity memoir. So they beeline to that book and purchase it; they might not have even ventured into the part of the store where you're sitting. Some bookstores may place a sign up front or outside to let people know there's a book signing happening. Some authors have their own signs bearing their name and the name of their book so readers know who they're approaching. Unless you're Casey McQuinston (and if you are . . . hi. Love your work.), people will almost certainly not know who you are on sight, so you need to tell them who you are and why you're here.

The more targeted the book signing, the better you'll do in terms of sales. For example, if you bring your children's book about being brave on the first day of school and set up shop outside your kid's school's kindergarten orientation, you *will* sell books. But if you just set up a table at a Barnes and Noble and wait, you might not get a lot of action.

It's a good idea to make your little table at a book signing as appealing as possible. If you've written a kids' book, put out some activities that will attract kids. Even something as simple as coloring pages and crayons will indicate to children that whatever's going on over here is for them. If you've written a science fiction book, perhaps some cool table decorations will help to convey to passersby what your book is about.

It's also smart to bring small giveaways to book signings. Not everyone will be ready to drop twenty bucks on your book on the spot. But if you can give them a sticker with your logo or a book-mark with your book's ordering information on it, you increase the odds that they'll recognize your book the next time they see it, which increases the likelihood that they'll opt to purchase it eventually in the future.

Readings

A book reading is a step up from a book signing, as surely you would also sign and sell books at an in-person reading. At a book reading, you would show up early to set up a little table before your allotted reading time, and then you'd read your book or a selection from your book to attendees. Then, afterward, you would hang out at your table, selling and signing books and connecting with the people who came to see you.

One downside to book readings is that people sometimes attend book readings as a free event, meaning they're not interested in purchasing the book, only in hearing you speak. That's better than them not being interested in buying your book *or* hearing you speak, and again, if you can get a bookmark in their hands, they may remember you and purchase later. But, for example, if you read your kids' book at story time at the library, you will likely not get many sales. People do not come to the public library expecting to spend money; the library is a place for community. If you go into an event like this not expecting book sales but expecting to build your community, you'll likely be happy in the end.

Both readings and signings often take place in bookstores or other small venues. You're doing the event there hoping to make some book sales. The venue is doing the event hoping for the same. You are hoping to benefit from their platform and venue; they are hoping you will bring them customers, whether they're selling books or toys or coffee or cocktails.

With these kinds of events, you need to bring your own audience, especially if you want to do more events with that venue in the future. You want them to be excited to have you, to feel that you are a valuable connection, to feel that you respect their time and energy. Do everything you can to promote this event in your personal network, online, and in your community ahead of time.

Festivals

There are lots of different kinds of book festivals. Some are small, while some are massive. Some are outdoor, some are indoor. Some are in the back room of your local brewery. Book festivals are happening all the time all over the place; your job is to figure out which ones are local to you, see if you can afford to participate, and attend when and if you can.

Often, book festivals feature booths, meaning that you can pay a fee to reserve a table at which to sell your book. Typically, this will get you a six- or eight-foot-long plastic table and one or two chairs. The rest is up to you. You could bring banners, signs, a tablecloth, decorations, containers, shelves—whatever you need to make your book exciting and your table on brand. If the festival is outside, and the organizers aren't providing this, you'll certainly want to bring a sunshade (which sometimes must also be a rainshade).

Many book festivals also feature book readings, interviews, and panel discussions[23]. You may be able to sign up or apply to participate in one or more of these kinds of events at a festival. You'll have to check out each festival's website or contact their organizer to learn more about what events are going on during the festival and how you can participate.

FUN FACT

There is a huge range in the prices that festivals charge to reserve a booth. Some are quite affordable, while others can be prohibitively expensive. While it's important to invest in your book's marketing, always only do what you can.

Some festivals aren't book festivals at all, but you can certainly sell books at them. Craft fairs and farmer's markets are great places to sell books, often without the competition of having thirty other authors there also peddling their wares. Always check out the guidelines for these events (when they're available) to see if you're allowed to sell books.

Conferences

Much like festivals, there are always writing conferences happening all over, and you'll need to do your own research to see which might be appropriate for you. Some conferences are huge, sponsored by international literary organizations, featuring Pu-

---

23   panel discussion: an event in which one interviewer, called a "moderator," interviews two or more people about a central topic or theme

litzer-prize-winning names. Some are smaller, intimate, local, and easier to participate in. Some you may be able to apply to speak at or participate in a panel at; others will be so big, you'll have to be content with paying for a ticket, attending, learning all you can, and making new connections. Some are broad, for all booklovers, whereas others are narrow, for historical romance writers only. Do some research to see what conferences are near you that you're interested in attending or speaking at, and then start taking steps to make that happen.

What to bring

Whatever kind of event you're doing, wherever you're doing it, you're going to want to bring a couple of things.

Copies of your book

Even if the venue or another vendor is selling copies of your book for you, there's a lot that could go wrong. They might not bring enough copies. Their credit card reader might die. They might get sick suddenly and have to run home. You don't want to not have copies of your book when people want to buy them.

A credit card reader

More on this on Page 223—but it's nearly impossible these days to sell a book without a credit card reader.

Promotional materials

Bring your branded bookmarks, business cards, and whatever else you got. If someone attends your event but doesn't buy a book, they need to walk away with some way to remember you. Maybe they'll come around and buy the book later. Maybe they'll leave your bookmark in a library book and the next person who reads it will find the bookmark and buy your book. You never know, and you never want someone to walk away from you without something to remember you by.

Email signup form

I know you have an email newsletter. If you don't, check Page 162.

Cool, so you've checked Page 162 and you now have an email newsletter. Bring a clipboard with a little chart or some other method where people can sign up for your email newsletter to stay in the loop about your future books and events.

Décor

If you're going to have a table or some other kind of station where people will be approaching you for books or autographs, you want it to look jazzy. Maybe the venue will have a nice table set up for you with a tablecloth and copies of your book already there. Maybe you have to bring all of that, including the table. Talk with the venue or other host ahead of time so you can bring exactly what you need—as well as some backups you might not need.

Other stuff

If you're a children's author, maybe you'll bring coloring pages or candy to attract children to your table. If you're a nonfiction author who wrote a book about pinecones, it's a good idea to have some pinecones on hand. There's a ton of other stuff you can bring, either to sell or just to get people interested in what you have to say.

Sales

For the most part, your book sales will come through online retailers and in-person retailers who have ordered your book from the distributor. That is to say, for the most part, you won't have to worry about literally *selling* your book at all. However, there are some instances in which you might want to or have to sell your book yourself, so here are some tips to make that process easier for you.

Selling books on your website

You may want to have an option on your website where people can purchase their book directly from you, and you'll send them a personalized package with a signed book and maybe some other cute accoutrements. Lots of authors opt not to do this, as it can be hard work. It involves collecting money, preparing the book and its packaging, and ultimately shipping that package, all in a timely manner. This also involves keeping a moderate stock of your books in your home and making sure you never run out, as you don't want a buyer to have to wait for you to purchase more books, receive the delivery, sign and package, and ship, and then also wait for that to be delivered to them.

But for those who do wish to do this, you absolutely can. You will need to place book orders through your publisher or your distributor regularly to ensure that you always have copies available for sale. From there, you can list on your website that people may purchase signed, personalized copies directly from you. You'll probably want to ask for their name (or the name of the person the book is for) as well as their shipping information. You can also hook up PayPal, Square, or another commerce platform to your website so people can purchase your book directly without you having to send them an invoice or anything funky.

The best way to integrate PayPal or another commerce platform will depend on what platform your website was created with, so be sure to speak with your website designer about this option. If you've designed your own website, there's likely a place where you can "add widgets" or "connect other apps" or similar, and there you'll see your options. You can also always search for blog posts or YouTube videos that will explain to you how best to sell on your website.

Selling books in person

You may need to sell books in person at an in-person event. If you're hosting an event at a bookstore, the odds are good that they'll want to sell books on your behalf. But there's a chance they're so small, their budget so tight, that they can't afford to do this. Or perhaps you're just too new, or your book too dissimilar from their typical audience, that they can't commit to the risk of purchasing copies.

If you're renting a booth at a festival or a conference, you'll definitely need to sell your own copies. These events rely on each creator or business to be able to independently take care of all their own needs, so you'll want to be prepared to make sales when you attend.

You may even need to sell books on the go! Imagine you make a new friend at your local brewery, and they're really interested in your book. Do you help them find the link and hope they purchase it later? Or do you run to the box of books you keep in your trunk for situations *just like this* and sell them a signed copy right then and there?

The answer is not cash. People don't reliably carry cash anymore, and they certainly don't carry exact change. You probably don't want to lug around a huge cash box either, though you can if you want to. Especially after the COVID-19 pandemic made people so hesitant about liberally exchanging goods that carry cooties, you will be expected to be able to accept credit card payments, and if you do not, you will lose sales.

There are plenty of programs that enable you to take credit card payments online, and you'll have to do some research and exploration to figure out which will work best for you. Many people and businesses use Square or another commerce platform similar to Square. A platform like Square will allow you to list several items—perhaps your paperback, your hardcover, and the branded T-shirts you're also selling—and ring people up easily. They'll send you a swipey thing so you can swipe, and perhaps a touch-reader thing so you can take touch cards, and they'll keep track of all your records so you can see your profits and other stats and easily file your taxes later.

However you do it, you need to be able to make sales in person, IRL, and you need to be able to take card sales at that. People will understand if you don't take cash (though it's easy to take cash, and platforms like Square help you ring in cash). People will not understand if you don't take cards.

The launch

We've talked about a lot of different marketing and publicity approaches so far in this book. But when do you do all of these things? When do they provide the most impact on book sales?

All of your publicity for your book will center around its launch. Your book launch is your due date for your book. It's your book's *day* of *birth*. It's the most exciting thing that will ever happen to your book. Your momentum will build and build and build up until this point; your launch day is when all that momentum pays off. People will *want* to be talking about it, so help them out! In the words of Bonnie Raitt, let's give 'em something to talk about.

The goal is for your book's publicity to look like this:

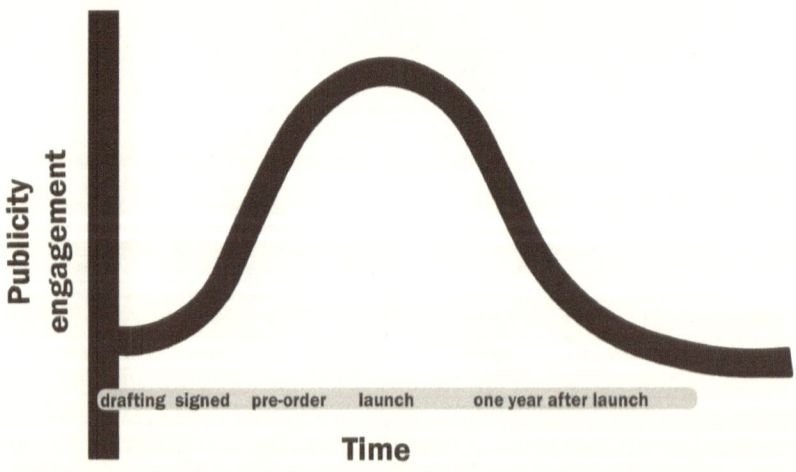

Note that this graphic never recommends zero publicity. You should be talking about your book the moment you think you might want to publish it, and you should never stop. As soon as you stop seeking publicity for your book, your book becomes old news.

When your book production is wrapping up and showing up in places on the internet as "coming soon" and "available for pre-order," you'll want to really rev up your publicity efforts. As your launch draws nearer and nearer, you'll want to be doing more and more events to drive those pre-orders.

On the day of your launch or perhaps on a weekend near your launch, you may choose to have a launch party. This can be a backyard affair with friends and family, or it can be a Zoom event with colleagues from around the world. But your launch day should also involve posting all over your social media platforms, some media features, and whatever else you can come up with!

FUN FACT

Most books are released on Tuesdays because the bestseller lists are posted on Tuesdays.

It's a good idea to get as many of your book reviewers, interviewers, and the rest of them to post about your book's release as close to its release date as possible. This places the majority of your hard-hitting publicity work squarely over your book's launch, which will drive a lot of sales right in those first few days. This will help your book rank higher in the search engines and get more notice by readers and book content creators alike.

FUN FACT

Social media users call a book's release date its #pubday.

After your book's launch, you will still be seeking publicity opportunities, though you will start to fall into a pattern, and your media appearances will likely slow a bit. Once your book launch is several months in the rearview mirror, it's time to settle into the steady rhythm of your marathon.

The marathon

Publishing a book is a marathon, not a sprint. The marathon starts the moment you write your first word, and it never truly ends. A successful author is constantly and consistently marketing themselves and their work in new and creative ways, as well as developing themselves professionally to seek new perspectives. They are always reaching out, looking for the next thing, always seeking a new project, a new audience, a new approach. An author's work is never over!

After your book has been produced, after its early publicity and pre-order, after its launch, and after your action-packed first couple of months, you will want to develop a method for keeping up your book's publicity while incorporating it into your other priorities or perhaps your next writing project. Aim for some publicity action every week or so, as the goal is for your book to never drop out of the conversation.

When you get a book review, author interview, or another media opportunity, you give people a reason to talk about your book. You have a new reason to post about your book on social media. You have something you can write about in a blog post. You have something your publisher and/or publicist can share to their networks. By constantly making sure your book is getting attention, you ensure it never leaves the spotlight.

People often ask, "How will I know if my book is successful?

How do you gauge success?" They're looking for a number of book sales to strive for. But numbers are abstract; you could tell an author to aim for any random number, and achieving that goal may mean success to some but failure to others. What really indicates success for an author and their book is diligence. An author who never gives up is a successful author. A book that is still being read, beloved, and talked about is a successful book. Most often, a book only fails to reach success when the author stops believing in it and stops prioritizing it. So prioritize your book. You have worked so hard and come so far; you deserve it.

Final thoughts

No one ever said making books is easy. It's hard. It takes a long time. It has lots of little moving parts. And once the book is done, no one will buy it unless you keep working, keep grinding, basically forever. The Amazon rainforest is dying; there's a paper and lumber shortage. People now own vast libraries on a single digital tablet. Making books is an act of supreme madness, and writers and editors can feel that madness pressing in as they work. But making books is also an act of radical empathy, radical expression, and passionate community building.

In order to be a successful author, you must be dedicated to your work. You must be willing to devote hours and hours of your life to drafting before you're even sure if anyone wants to publish it. You must be willing to listen to your editor and make changes because you trust that it will help you. You must be willing to wait on other people's creative energy and availability to provide clear, compassionate feedback. You must be willing to review review review, more times than you thought possible, until you cannot stand to look at your own book anymore. You must be willing to make spreadsheets, organize, and plan with no end in sight. You must be willing to make new friends and connections, and give as well as receive. You must be willing to do the work. That's the only way to become a successful author.

But you *can* do it, and it's going to be awesome! If you're still drafting or maybe only dreaming of drafting your first novel, all that you've read in this book probably feels extremely overwhelming. But you don't start with all of this. You start with getting your story into a Word document. You start by focusing on your story, and then you take the process step by step until you're here, at the end, where you will work a little bit forever at this thing you love so much and have poured so much of yourself into.

Start at the beginning. Go at your own pace. Do what you're comfortable with. Seek help. And never fear. Because it's going to be awesome.

Glossary

- **acquisitions editor:** an editor at a publishing company who is responsible for assessing manuscript submissions and making decisions on whether and how to publish them

- **adult book:** a book whose intended audience is eighteen and over

- **algorithm:** the elaborate codes each social media platform develops to process all their content, which decides what posts to show which people when, based on their personal data and other factors

- **art direction:** any guidance or reference you give to your illustrator

- **beta reader:** a person who will read your manuscript draft and provide feedback on areas that could be strengthened

- **the Big Five:** Penguin/Random House, Hachette Book Group, Harper Collins, Simon & Schuster, and Macmillan (some people include Amazon's self-publishing arm as a sixth "big" publisher)

- **brand:** being mindful of what content you're presenting, why you're presenting it, how you can best present it, and how that connects to who you are as a person; all the cool things that are important to you, presented in a way that makes you relatable and interesting to other people

- **casebound:** a hardcover book minus the dust cover, or the way such a book is bound
- **character description:** a written description of a character than an illustrator will use to produce an illustration of that character
- **character sketch**: the first illustration the illustrator does of a character
- **children's book:** a book whose intended audience is in grade school or younger (also called a juvenile book)
- **color illustration:** an illustration that has been colored and is final or in the process of being finalized
- **cooperative publishing:** a publishing track that involves a financial investment from both publisher and author, in which authors get to be very involved in the creative process and earn higher royalties to help recoup their investment
- **copy editing:** editing very closely for spelling, grammar, and mechanics
- **cover finish:** whether your book is glossy (shiny) or matte (not shiny)
- **cover price:** the price that is printed on your book's cover (which retailers may choose to discount)
- **designer:** the person who lays out the interior of your book and creates the cover layout; they or another designer may also design marketing materials and other graphics

- **developmental editing:** editing to develop your overall story in terms of plot, character, consistency, worldbuilding, layout, and/or titles
- **digital art:** art produced on a computer or other device
- **digital printing:** a printing method in which the printer takes a book's digital file and simply prints the number of copies requested, sort of like a high-quality computer printer, rather than setting a physical printer
- **distributor:** a company responsible for taking your completed book from your printer and distributing it to retailers
- **editor:** the person who is reviewing your book with the intention of making changes or recommendations regarding story, theme, characters, syntax, clarity, grammar, spelling, and other mechanics; also, any person in the publishing industry who performs any editorial work (for example, an acquisitions editor)
- **elevator pitch:** a one-sentence summary of your book that is designed to really hook someone hearing about it for the first time in as few words as possible
- **endorsement:** a book review you get before your book is out or even complete for the purpose of putting it on the cover or interior of the book itself
- **feature:** when a reviewer or another journalist or influencer covers your book, but has perhaps not read it and refrains from making review-type commentary on it; when any publication or creator posts about your book in a way that is not a review and not an interview

- **fiction:** a type of book whose story is fabricated, even if it's grounded in real life events
- **format:** the type of book your book is (hardcover, paperback, audiobook, e-book, etc.)
- **glossy:** shiny (in book world, usually referring to a book cover)
- **handle:** the username people can search for to find you on social media, usually starting with an @
- **illustrator:** a person who draws pictures for use in a book
- **illustration:** an image to be placed inside a book along with text or used on the cover
- **illustration description:** a written description of how an illustration should look for the illustrator to use in producing said illustration
- **imprint:** the brand name under which books are published (may be the publishing company's name, like Penguin Random House, or may be one of the publishing company's smaller imprints, like PRH's Bantam Books)
- **independent publisher:** a publishing company that is not affiliated with the Big Five, Amazon, or another major corporation
- **International Standard Book Number (ISBN):** a number unique to your book that helps libraries and retailers keep track of it
- **interview:** an article or post in which the focus is the publication or creator asking you questions and reflecting on your answers
- **layout:** the placement of text, images, and other design elements

- **Library of Congress Control Number (LCCN):** a number the Library of Congress gives you in exchange for registering your book with them (US only)
- **line editing:** editing to review line-by-line language choices, complex grammar, and semantics
- **literary agent:** an employee of a literary agency who seeks out books and authors they feel are marketable and unique and then connects those books and authors with publishing companies
- **manuscript:** the text of a book before it's designed into a book layout, from the moment the author starts writing it to the completion of the final proofread
- **matte:** not shiny (in book world, usually referring to a book cover)
- **mechanics:** punctuation, spelling, and capitalization
- **media:** the type of material used in producing an illustration (pencil, digital, fabric, etc.) or news outlets that may publicize your book
- **memoir:** a type of book that recounts part or all of the author's life
- **metadata:** all of the information about your book, like its contributors, LCCN and IBSN(s), keywords, BISAC codes, THEMA codes, synopsis, etc.
- **middle grade book:** a book whose intended audience is approximately in middle school, or around nine to thirteen years old

- **nonfiction:** a type of book that is factual and in no part fabricated
- **query:** the process of sending your manuscript and accompanying submission materials to one or more agents or publishers in hopes that they will offer to represent or publish it (can be a noun, "the query [email or package]," or a verb, "to query")
- **offer:** a publisher's or agent's specific terms under which they propose to publish or represent you
- **offset printing:** a printing method in which the printing press is physically set to your book's design, rendering very high-resolution images and often involving the printing of a thousand or more copies at a time
- **one-page illustration:** an illustration that takes up the entirety of one single page of a book from top to bottom, from edge to crease
- **packager:** a publishing company or another service that facilitates the author self-publishing their own book. Some are full service, while others (like Amazon) are more click-it-and-get-done, you're-on-your-own.
- **panel discussion:** an event in which one interviewer, called a "moderator," interviews two or more people about one topic or theme
- **paper weight:** the thickness of paper, often referring to interior book pages
- **picture book:** a children's book that features pictures as a main part of the story

- **pre-marketing:** marketing you can do for yourself as an author and your book before the book is scheduled for release
- **pre-order:** the sale of copies of your book in advance of its release date
- **print release:** a document an author signs acknowledging that they believe their book is ready to go to print
- **printer:** a company that physically prints books
- **printer's proof:** a single print copy of a book, typically produced in each of its formats, so the author and publisher can ensure that every element looks the same in real life as it did on the computer
- **production:** the entire process of publishing your book from its first edit to its final proof review
- **project manager:** the publisher's employee whose job it is to oversee your book's production and keep track of its many moving parts
- **proof:** a full copy of your book at its current stage in production, from a raw Word file to a finished and printed copy of your book
- **proofread:** a final review of your book that seeks to correct only glaring errors regarding spelling, grammar, and mechanics
- **publisher:** a company or organization that prepares content (in our case, books) for distribution to the public

- **query letter:** a brief (no longer than a page) and concise cover letter for your manuscript submission that usually includes your genre, intended audience, word count, synopsis, and may need to include other details depending on the publisher or agent you are querying
- **retailer:** a business that sells products (in this case, your book)
- **review:** when a reviewer or publication receives a copy of your book (often for free), reads it, and then writes a blurb about their thoughts
- **royalty:** a percentage of the profit that the author will earn per each book sold
- **royalty structure:** the threshold (in number of copies) at which you start earning a percentage of the profits from your book sales, and then the subsequent thresholds at which that percentage increases
- **self-publishing:** the author acting as the publisher of their own book by either doing the work themselves or hiring people to do some or all of the work per their vision
- **simultaneous submissions:** queries made to more than one publisher or agent at the same time
- **sketch:** a first concept for an illustration, often rendered in black and white, to establish layout, content, and other elements

- **slush pile:** the queue of submissions an agent or publisher has yet to evaluate. This term comes from the olden days, when they'd have real towers of actual paper manuscripts stacked all over their offices. Now, the slush pile refers to the digital queue of submissions.
- **soft proof (or digital proof):** a PDF file of how your book will print that authors and designers can review to confirm that everything was received correctly by the printer
- **spot illustration:** a small illustration that typically features only one or two characters and little to no background
- **standard manuscript format:** a generally agreed-upon set of formatting guidelines that most publishers prefer manuscripts be submitted in
- **synopsis:** summary
- **tracking changes:** any program in a word processor that allows you to keep track of your edits easily as you make changes to your manuscript
- **traditional art:** manual, non-digital art media including paints, pencils, etc.
- **traditional publishing:** a publishing track in which the publisher invests one hundred percent of the production funds, but in which an author is much less involved in the production process
- **trim size:** the dimensions of your book head-on (ie. not including the spine)

- **two-page illustration (or a "two-page spread"):** an illustration that covers the entirety of two facing pages of a book, from top to bottom, across the center crease

- **uncorrected galley:** a version of your book that is in the design process but not yet complete

- **unsolicited manuscript:** a manuscript submission that a publisher has not explicitly requested from an author or agent

- **vanity publishing:** publication of a book for a fee with no regard for its craft or content

- **vignette:** an illustration that typically features a small scene with a couple of characters, a limited background, and a fade or other border that does not reach the edges of the page

- **young adult book:** a book whose intended audience is around fourteen to eighteen, though this genre is embraced universally by adults (often rendered as YA)

Standard Manuscript Format Sample

Indie Book Publishing from Start to Finish:

It's Going to Be Awesome

by Christina Kann

Introduction

So you wrote a book. Well done! That is truly the hardest part, and you've done it and now it's done. That's amazing! You might be ready to sit back and wipe your hands clean of it all, but if you want to get published, your work is nowhere near over.

From a publishing perspective, you haven't even gotten started yet. That an author has written a book is a given in the publishing world; what matters is how that book transforms in the publishing process and where it ends up once it's published. Of course, it matters that you wrote the book. But who you work with to publish your book, how they make your book better, where your book is sold, the profit you can make, and the readers who are impacted by the book also matter.

If you aren't interested in enacting someone's else's recommendations for bettering and selling your book, that's totally fine! That makes you a perfect candidate for self-publishing, and you'll still want to consider a lot of these steps along the way. On the flip side, maybe you've received an offer from a big traditional publisher. Congrats! Most of the steps of this book will take place at the publisher, and you may not get to see much of it, but this book can still serve as important context for what is happening behind the curtain. Maybe you've received a cooperative or traditional publishing offer from an indie publisher who wants to publish your book traditionally or cooperatively. That's awesome too! In that case, you'll definitely want to read this book carefully and take heed of the advice it has to offer.

Query Letter Sample

Christina Kann
christina@wildlingpress.com
(804)YOU-WISH

Dear Ms. Ball,

I'm writing to submit my 50,000-word nonfiction book about independent book publishing for your consideration. *Indie Book Publishing from Start to Finish: It's Going to Be Awesome!* is a clear, straightforward guide to self- and independent publishing targeted toward beginners in an attempt to demystify much of the process. As I'm sure you know, there is much gatekeeping in this historic industry, and my aim aligns with Wilding's: I want to level the playing field and make book publishing accessible to everyone.

As the title suggests, my book is a comprehensive guide that walks new authors through the entire publishing process, from the moment they finish their first draft through to their long-term marketing plan. This is unique in the marketplace, where many books about writing focus on either the writing or the marketing, and often on niche topics within these broader subjects. The goal is for authors to come away from this book with an understanding of the scope of work they will have to go through to publish and market their book, and then they can do more detailed research on the individual tasks on their own (with some guidance from my recommended additional reading at the end!).

At Wildling, you've made it clear that you're committed to uplifting marginalized voices and making publishing more accessible to those whose voices have historically not been heard. This book will serve as a tool to those people who haven't had other opportunities to learn about publishing—perhaps even other Wildling authors someday?

Thank you so much for your time and consideration. I'm really hoping we can work together!

Best,

Christina Kann
christina@wildlingpress.com

Additional resources

Podcasts

- *How Do I Book?* hosted by Wildling Press (writing, production, marketing, reading)

- *The Book Action Marketing Podcast* hosted by Becky Robinson (marketing)

- *All Things Book Marketing* hosted by Smith Publicity (marketing)

- *Book Marketing Tips and Author Success* hosted by Penny Sansevieri and Amy Cornell (marketing)

- *Publishing Profits* hosted by Tom Corson-Knowles (marketing)

Books

- *Reach: Create the Biggest Possible Audience for Your Message, Book, or Cause* by Becky Robinson (marketing)

- *Steering the Craft* by Ursula K. Le Guin (writing and revising)

- *Save the Cat! Writes a Novel* by Jessica Brody

Additional resources, cont.

Blogs

- *The Storygrid* by Shaun Coyne (writing and editing)

- Helping Writers Become Authors
  www.helpingwritersbecomeauthors.com
  (writing and editing)

- Jane Friedman www.janefriedman.com (publishing business
  with some writing and editing)

About the Author

photo by Jason Hilton / IG @negativeselections

Christina Kann is a lifelong reader and writer with a special interest in clever science fiction and fantasy. Her greatest strengths are that her confidence is too high and she can keep talking forever, against all odds. She's obsessed with the color pink and flowers and cats and sociolinguistics and gardening. She founded Deus Ex Media podcast network and hosts Burn Before Reading, a podcast about the cringeworthy stuff we wrote when we were kids. She lives in the beautiful city of Richmond, Virginia, with her steadfast husband, Sean, and their four cats: Penny, Dante, Pepper, and Korra.

Christina Kann, Author

@christinakann_

@christinakann

www.ingramcontent.com/pod-product-compliance
Lightning Source LLC
Chambersburg PA
CBHW021616120626
46545CB00001B/263